SWIMMING

SWIMMING

BY

MONTAGUE A. HOLBEIN

WITH ILLUSTRATIONS

TWENTY-SECOND THOUSAND

BLOOMSBURY

First published 1914 under the title *Swimming* by C. Arthur Pearson Limited

Copyright © 2005 Octopus Publishing Group

This edition published by Bloomsbury Publishing in 2005

The moral right of the author has been asserted

Bloomsbury Publishing Plc, 36 Soho Square, London W1D 3QY

A CIP catalogue record for this book is available from the British Library

ISBN 0 7475 7908 3
ISBN-13 9780747579083

10 9 8 7 6 5 4 3 2 1

Printed by Clays Ltd, St Ives plc

All papers used by Bloomsbury Publishing are natural, recyclable products
made from wood grown in well-managed forests. The manufacturing processes
conform to the environmental regulations of the country of origin.

http://www.bloomsbury.com

It is advisable to check with your doctor before embarking on any exercise
programme. A physician should be consulted in all matters relating to health.
Neither the author nor the publisher can accept legal responsibility
for any injury sustained while following the exercises.

Contents

Preface

EVERY one ought to know how to swim. We are a nation of sailors, are proud of everything that appertains to the seas that wash our shores, and yet swimming is an art, even to-day, which is strangely neglected.

Swimming should be cultivated by all Britons, not only as an acquirement that may be called into operation for the saving of life, but also as a means for the development of muscular strength.

If it were generally known that swimming is highly beneficial to the nervous system, and repairs the vital functions when a person is falling into a decline, it is safe to say that many of those thus afflicted would at once determine to learn and practice it.

Happily there is a disposition throughout the country to add constantly to the number of swimming baths at present in existence. Still we are lamentably behind the Continental nations in recognising that every boy and girl at an early age should be compelled to learn.

I do not mean to say that Britons are not fond of the water—far from it. The reverse, in fact, is the case. A visit to any watering-place in the summer season will soon

Why Animals Swim Naturally

convince any one that the people of this kingdom delight to take a "dip" whenever it is possible.

But what I must lament is the deplorable number of people who are content to paddle in the shallows—afraid to go a foot out of their depth. For one bather who can swim you will find thirty who cannot.

I wonder how many amidst the crowds who watched me land from my cross-channel swim could fearlessly have swum one hundred yards with me in the currents ten miles out.

I do not intend to dilate at length on the great benefits of swimming. All common-sense folk ought to be aware, by a natural intuition, of its advantages to health—to life itself. Neither am I going to give any account of its rise and progress. Such information is of little value to the novice, and when the novice becomes an expert, if he is so minded he can easily acquire the history of swimming at the nearest library.

Lack of confidence is the only thing which prevents thousands of people from the attempt. Strange to say, too, in my experience I have found that the "timid sex"—the ladies—learn to swim much more quickly than men. Who will say that they lack confidence after this?

Nearly every animal can swim naturally on finding itself in the water for the first time. Man cannot, and these are the reasons:—

A dog, when swimming, adopts the same position, or nearly so, which it would assume if it were walking in the street. The action of its limbs, therefore, when swimming, are the same as when it is walking. It has, consequently, nothing to learn when it falls or is even thrown into the water

Importance of Good Style

for the first time. Man, on the contrary, has to abandon his usual erect position, and has to manipulate his limbs in an unaccustomed manner.

In learning to swim the novice must regard his body as a boat, and his arms and legs as sculls. On the proper use of these his successful propulsion through the water will depend.

At the outset I cannot too strongly impress upon would-be swimmers that a good style must be aimed at. Bad habits acquired at the beginning are hard to unlearn—in fact, sometimes can never be corrected. Readers will be warned against such errors at the proper times and places.

Don't strive for pace first, but bear in mind that when style has been acquired pace will follow as a matter of course.

I have heard wondrous tales amongst clubmen and others of how certain individuals have learned to swim at their first attempt. This has induced many to attempt to learn. They have perhaps assumed a forced confidence, and boldly plunged into the water, only to find that they have at once sunk like a stone, despite all their struggles, and generally had a most unpleasant time before being hauled out.

Not desiring a second experience, they conceive that they have been hoaxed, and at once give up the attempt to learn.

Such tales do more harm than good.

There always has been and always will be a considerable difference in the time that various people will take in learning to swim.

I hope, however, after a perusal of this book, and armed with the necessary confidence, it will only be a matter of hours for the average boy or girl to be at home in and to move easily through the water.

CHAPTER I

AIDS TO SWIMMING

MANY and various are the so-called "aids to swimming." Although I have carefully examined dozens of them, I cannot conscientiously say that a single one has been brought under my notice that I would have given six-pence for.

When the novice is learning he is almost certain to get the idea into his head that he will be able to swim so much more easily if he has a body-belt of cork round him, or perhaps some air-bladders tied under his neck; or it may be he will have brought to his notice a wonderful pair of fin-gloves that will enable him to paddle through the water like a duck. Even if the learner does not think of any such things himself, there is almost certain to be somebody who knew some one who once learned to swim by artificial means, and the tyro will perhaps be induced to buy some such patent aids to swimmers.

Patent Devices for Learning not Desirable.

It is quite true such contrivances will keep one afloat, but not in a thousand years will they ever teach or enable any one to swim.

Sometimes they are even a positive danger to life.

Suppose, for instance, you were learning to swim by such

methods in a river or the open sea. With a body-belt or bladders attached to your person you would be in an upright position in the water, but not in the necessary attitude for swimming. The current of the river or the waves might gradually drift you from the shore without your perceiving it for some time, and knowing little or nothing about propelling yourself through the water, you might be hopelessly carried away before assistance could arrive. And all this would have been brought about through the agency of an " aid to swimmers."

To become a good musician you must first go through all the drudgery of those troublesome " scales." There is no drudgery in the initial stages of learning to swim, but certain obstacles have to be surmounted, and that done all is plain sailing.

I remember many years ago a young friend of mine was very enthusiastic over some pneumatic apparatus that his brother had patented, and with its aid he determined to learn to swim.

The device was a kind of cycle tube that ran along both arms and once round the chest.

The youth entered the water with the utmost confidence, accompanied by a friend who could swim fairly well. The latter had agreed to give him any instructions that were necessary.

Everything went well until the young man had cheerfully waded out of his depth. Then, to the horror and consternation of his companion, directly his feet left the ground the experimenter with his brother's patent turned upside down, and in place of his head only his feet could be seen frantically kicking above the water.

Of course not a moment was lost in rescuing him from his

unenviable position, but that patent was at once relegated to the region where the majority of such " inventions " and " aids " ought to be—the dust-bin.

The Duly Effective Aid in Learning.

There is only one effective aid to swimming that I can honestly recommend—and too much of that even is not good.

Get a girdle of webbing from a saddler's shop. This should be about six inches wide, and be fastened round the chest by a strong buckle. See that it is strapped high up under the armpits. Attach to this belt a stout cord, and run this through a hole in a pole that is secured across the footpath and projects over the bath.

The services of a friend must be requisitioned, who, by means of the rope, is able " to play " the swimmer, and prevent him from sinking.

This method does not hamper the movements of the man in the water. It perpetually keeps his head constantly above water, and the friend can use his discretion in relaxing his hold of the cord.

Gradually the swimmer by following the instructions given him by the teacher will learn to keep himself afloat by his own exertions, and immediately this is found to be the case the girdle should be discarded.

This treatment, of course, is only possible whilst learning to swim in a bath. There are other aids which may be permitted to the learner in river waters or the sea.

Learning with a Girdle.

At this point I may as well acquaint the novice with what he should do when learning to swim in a bath with the support of a girdle.

First Arm Movement

Throw your head well back until the chin rests on the water, curve your body, keep your legs well together, so that the knees and ankles touch. Let your toes stretch as far back as possible. Now press your hands firmly together, and you are ready to start.

First Arm Movement.

Extend your arms to the front until they are perfectly horizontal with the rest of your body. Keep them below the surface of the water.

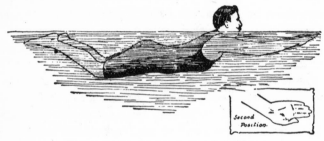

Breast Stroke—First and Second Positions.

Turn your wrists inwards until the knuckles of both hands are in a line with and touching each other.

Second Arm Movement.

Keep the arms perfectly rigid, then sweep them outwards and backwards very slowly, until the tips of the fingers are at right angles to the body.

Third Arm Movement.

Now press the hands inwards and slightly downwards, draw in the elbows, and as the latter touch your sides let

Third Arm Movement

your hands, pointed forwards, come together under the chin. Keep your fingers well together, your legs rigid, and make every movement slowly.

When you have practised these three movements a little while you will find that you will be moving forward in the

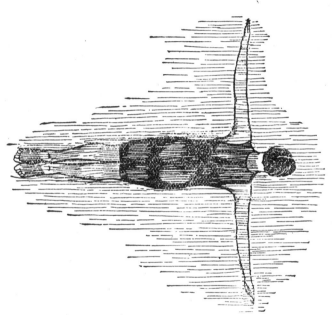

Breast Stroke—Third Position.

water. When this auspicious moment arrives you may then—but on no account before—attempt to use your legs.

Now you have to combine the movements you have already learnt with those that belong to the legs.

The Leg Movement.

The first leg movement consists in bending both knees, and drawing them outwards at the moment of extending both the arms.

Now open the legs as widely as possible with a vigorous kick.

This backward sweep should bring the legs together when extended to their full length.

When your ankles touch, your hands should be outwards.

Breast Stroke—Fourth Position.

Draw your legs up again, and as your hands come up under your chin, repeat the leg movement backwards as before.

That, then, is practically the only reliable aid to swimming that can be given in a bath.

A Swimmer Friend.

The best aid that a novice can have when learning in the river or the sea is a friend who can swim well. This friend

A Swimmer Friend

is indeed a friend in need, and as the young beginner strikes off will hold the tip of his finger to the tip of the learner's chin, thus keeping his head above water and giving the right instructions in the meantime as to leg and arm movements.

Another way is for a friend to precede the swimmer in a small boat, and throw a rope to the learner, who places it under his arms; this keeps him afloat until he is able to manage for himself.

There are many other "aids," as I have before remarked, but as I believe in none of them, I do not propose to discuss their merits or demerits in this work.

If the young swimmer be nervous he will get more real assistance from a friend who can swim than he will from a heap of patent contrivances.

CHAPTER II

MAKING A START

Where to Bathe.

ALTHOUGH many novices do not credit it, the best place to learn to swim is in the open sea.

This is accounted for by the fact that sea water, being so much heavier than fresh, gives more support to the body, and thus enables the beginner to float much sooner than ever he can expect to do in fresh water. Another advantage is in the fact that salt water being so nauseous to the taste, the learner takes very good care to keep his mouth tightly closed, thus at once preventing himself from falling into the common error of opening it as he swims.

At the riverside or the seashore the best place for learning to swim from is where there is a gradually sloping sandy or gravelly shore. The spot should be entirely free from holes, weeds, and stones, and where river swimming is contemplated, a muddy bottom is to be avoided.

When to Bathe.

Delicate persons should never bathe before breakfast; between 10 a.m. and noon is the best time of the day for such people to swim.

Those who do go for a "dip before breakfast" should eat a biscuit before entering the water. This, bear in mind, is

Entering the Water

no permission to eat a hearty meal, which is a most harmful practice just prior to a swim at any time of the day.

Do not go into the water when you feel cold, when you feel hot, when you have a headache, or when it is raining.

If the place selected for your initial attempt is near houses, look to see if any broken glass or crockery is lying about. Such fragments inflict nasty wounds if trodden upon.

A Rope Useful.

When swimming either in a river, a canal, a pond, or the sea, it is as well to provide oneself with a tolerably long Manilla rope. This can be fastened to something firmly on shore, and the lightness of the rope causing it to float upon the water, it is always handy "in case of accidents," which will occur, as you know, in the best of well-regulated families.

You can even go one better than this, and tie your rope —one about the thickness of a clothes line will suffice— to a small plank and take it out into the stream with you.

Entering the Water.

Now enter the water.

Wade in quietly, without any hurry or anxiety, until the water reaches your waist. Stop here and just paddle about for a moment or so. This will give you confidence and get you used to the feel of the water. Turn your face to the shore, grip your rope tightly, and suddenly bob down, immersing yourself completely.

Don't shirk it—go right under. Many a man who does this for the first time is ready to swear that he has gone quite three feet under the surface, when in reality the water has only got into his nose, mouth, and ears, *and the back of his head is dry !*

Gaining Confidence

This is the way to duck : put your left hand on the top of your head, grip the rope with your right, then go right down until you feel that your left hand is completely under water.

Then come up, puff and blow, try to wipe the water out of your eyes with your wet hands, and generally enjoy yourself for a moment or two. There is no hurry.

Gaining Confidence in the Buoyancy of the Water.

Now jump up and down a bit and you will learn that the water is buoyant. This fact will make you reflect that it requires very little effort on your part to keep yourself afloat. Move about as much as you like in the water, but don't leave go of the rope yet.

In fact I would strongly recommend that the first time of entering the water should be entirely devoted to making oneself confident about wading in up to the chin.

A good beginning in everything is invaluable, and especially is this the case in swimming.

A person who is unaccustomed to the water, finding himself gradually wading into deeper depths with every two or three inches he advances, is apt to feel qualms on the subject of his safety whether an able swimmer be in the vicinity or not. It is as well, therefore, that of his own accord he should gradually, after having taken the preliminary ducking, make his own way of his own inclination into deeper water.

To feel a perfect confidence of the sustaining power of the element in which he finds himself, the learner will do well, before he attempts to swim, to learn first of all to float on the back.

This most important subject deserves a chapter to itself.

CHAPTER III

FLOATING

EVEN when one has become a good swimmer, floating is always a useful, enjoyable, and graceful pastime.

Wade out from the shore until the water reaches up to the armpits. With your back to the bank, bend your knees until the water touches your chin. Keep your mouth shut. Put your head well back gradually until the base of the skull is immersed and you feel the water actually in your ears.

Then slowly extend your arms backwards behind your head as far as ever they will go, the palms being uppermost.

Take a deep breath, fill your lungs well, and you will be greatly surprised to find that your legs, as you stiffen and separate them, actually want to rise to the surface of the water of their own accord. Let them do so.

Throw your head still further back, elevate your nose and chin, and in this position you may float at pleasure.

Keep your lungs inflated.

Directly you attempt to take in breath you will commence to sink, so you must be quick about it—both in the acts of expelling and drawing in again. You will not sink so rapidly but that the quick respiration will restore the equilibrium before the water reaches the nose.

The main difficulty about floating is that, do as one will

The Theory of Floating

at first, the legs won't rise; but I think that if my advice given above is closely followed, it will be found generally successful.

The value of this branch of swimming cannot be over-estimated, and I have no hesitation in recommending my readers to practise floating for some time before they try to swim, as this, and this alone, will give them perfect confidence that if they assume a correct attitude the water cannot fail to support them.

Floating.

The Theory of Floating.

A little theory at this juncture may be of service more fully to explain why I am hammering at this particular topic.

A human being weighs very much less than water. It goes without saying that the lighter substance will float in the denser. Consequently man, woman, or child *must* be able to float in water.

If a person were to faint in the river his shoulders would appear above the surface of the water, but none of his head

The Theory of Floating

would be seen. This is explained by the fact that the head, being a solid mass of brain, bone, and muscle, and much heavier than water, would sink as a matter of course, but the lungs, being filled with air, would buoy up the shoulders. The rest of the body and the limbs would fall forward, and the body would turn round until only the back was exposed to view.

This fact is the key to man's method of swimming. But nobody can breathe through his shoulders, so the head has to be held above water somehow.

Keep your mouth and nostrils above water, and you will inhale and exhale as much air as you want.

Floating.

The nostrils are set in the heaviest part of the whole body, so remember that your hardest task will be to keep your head continuously above water.

In floating, the entire position of the body will be reversed. The learner will be upon his back, his spine will be arched, and the heaviest part of man, the back of the head, will be partly supported by the water and partly by the air in the lungs. ˙ By this means the nostrils will become the lightest part of the learner, and be above the surface of the water when the remainder of the body and limbs are submerged.

27

The Theory of Floating

When floating, the learner will find that when he expels a breath his face will sink as far as the eyebrows and the lower lip, but the nostrils and the mouth will remain above water. Directly, however, air is inhaled the entire face rises out of the water.

CHAPTER IV

THE A B C OF SWIMMING

UNDOUBTEDLY the A B C of natation is learning the strokes by which the body is propelled, while the head is not allowed to sink below the surface.

What I have already described and advised the beginner to learn, such as ducking, wading, and floating, may be likened to the pothooks and hangers one learns at school before the teacher starts the pupil on the alphabet. They all lead up to the main thing.

Somebody once said that a man's actions when swimming resembled those of a frog. This is utterly absurd. The limbs of the man and of the reptile are differently formed, and it is impossible for them to be worked in the same manner. Therefore such an idea may be dismissed at once.

Practising the First Strokes with the Arms.

Now when you desire to practise the first strokes, enter the water until you are immersed up to the armpits. Then turn your face towards the bank.

Stretch out your arms before you at full length, keeping the palms of the hands flat downwards. Take a long breath, get your head back as far as possible, and gently push your nose in the direction of the shore.

Practising the First Leg Strokes

This will start you.

Your feet will leave the ground, and you will feel very much inclined to go under altogether. Resisting this idea with all your might, spread your arms out slowly and deliberately, keeping them below the surface of the water always, until the tips of your fingers are on a level with your shoulders.

That is enough for the first attempt—let your feet touch the bottom again.

Repeat this action time after time, and at each attempt you will find yourself nearer the bank.

Practising the First Leg Strokes.

Now it is only fair that the legs should do a share in the propulsion of your body shoreward, and you will find them very willing and able assistants if you only get them to recognise that you are their master.

They will endeavour to *master you* at first, bear that in mind.

I will assume that you have sufficiently acquired the elementary arm stroke to attempt using the legs.

As you shoot out your hands for the half-circular stroke, raise your feet from the bottom, bend both knees, drawing them well outwards. Then, with a smart kick out, open your legs to their widest extent.

Depress your heels, contract your toes upwards, turn both your feet to right angles. Describe a semicircle with each leg until your legs come together again in a straight line with your body.

The power of this stroke does not depend so much on the kick as on the determination with which the legs are drawn together. This action, in itself, forces the water out from between the legs, and so impels the body forward.

The natural inclination is to hump the back. This must be resisted, because you want to drive the body forward and not out of the water.

As you did when practising the arm stroke, after having made the first attempt drop your feet to the bottom. Then in a moment repeat the action quietly. Remember, there is no hurry.

After a time you will find that you can combine the arm and leg actions quite nicely, but possibly some little difficulty will be experienced with your breathing apparatus.

When to Breathe.

You are trying hard to obey instructions—to keep your mouth closed—but the wretched water somehow will find the way into your mouth and nostrils.

A beginner always draws in his breath just at the moment he strikes out. This ensures the getting his mouth and nostrils full of water at once, and a collapse is inevitable.

If you will remember to take breath between the strokes, all will be well. Quite naturally when you draw your knees outwards for the kick you will inhale, and just as surely as your feet are thrust from you, will you expel the air from your lungs. Knowledge on the management of the breath will come with practice, and can only be acquired in that one way.

Improving the Strokes.

When you have practised the arm and leg strokes, which, of course, are alternate—first arms, then legs, arms again,

Improving the Strokes

out with your knees, and so on—these movements may be strengthened and perfected by making the motions as continuous and machine-like as possible.

Further, the arms, acting like sculls, should be made to come round with a steady, strong sweep, the fingers and thumbs being kept perfectly tight, and the palms hollowed.

Always remember, however, to perfect one movement thoroughly before proceeding to the next.

CHAPTER V

THE BREAST STROKE

I WILL now assume that my readers have mastered the foregoing instructions, in which case they can confidently say that they have done all the hard work there is to be done in swimming; the rest is all pleasure. For if you can manage half a dozen consecutive strokes, it will be no hardship to you to do a hundred, always provided you are not in a very great hurry.

Having learnt the breast stroke in shallow water, your next effort should be to try it in the deep—*i.e.*, out of your depth.

Attempt this when you can take about six arm and leg strokes in succession in shallow water.

Wade into deep water as far as you can go and take a couple of strokes into yet deeper parts. The knowledge that you cannot touch the bottom may be alarming at first, but keep perfectly cool, and remember instructions. Let these excursions into the danger zone be short at first, and only take longer advances as you feel that practice has made you perfect.

Lie Low in the Water.

The swimmer must always lie as low as possible in the water, remembering that if he only places a finger-tip above the surface he is adding a weight to that which he has to keep afloat.

33   C

The Side Stroke

All beginners are extremely anxious to keep their nostrils well above water. In doing this many press their hands downwards. This at once raises the head and neck, and sometimes even the chest, out of the element in which they should be submerged. This needlessly tires the arms, and besides develops "bad form," for a high and showy swimmer may be likened to a high-stepping horse. There is no endurance in either.

One can never be an expert swimmer, however, with

Side Stroke.

a knowledge of the breast stroke alone. In a long swim, for instance, the tension thrown on the muscles of the neck is very considerable; consequently other means have to be resorted to to relieve the monotony. Besides, the chest and shoulders offer so much resistance to the water that anything like substantial progress is very much retarded.

The Side Stroke.

Therefore the knowledge of how to swim on the side should be next acquired, as being a very valuable step in

The Side Stroke

substantial swimming progress, and also because it should be next in order as a lesson.

You can swim on your left or your right sides—as you choose. As a matter of fact you should be able to do both at will, and as occasion requires.

Strangely enough, instructors now rarely teach the side stroke—it has, I suppose, gone out of fashion. Why, I could never understand.

To acquire this stroke read carefully:

Side Stroke—First Position.

The best way to acquire this stroke, which is practically the breast stroke adapted to the side, is to begin with the legs. Hold the steps of the bath with your hands in such a manner as to incline the body on either side. Slightly lift the knee of the top leg, then with an outward movement straighten it. At the same time make a similar movement with the under leg, except that it must be made to work backwards. Now the legs must be brought sharply together.

The Side Stroke

When you have thoroughly grasped the leg movement, it will be time to acquire the arm stroke. Particular attention must be paid to the work of the under arm, the proper use of which prevents stopping between the stroke.

The under arm must be extended in a straight line with the palm of the hand upwards, and in the downward movement the palm should be reversed, and brought to the pit of the stomach. The upper arm commences the stroke as the under one finishes; in this case the left is extended in a line with the nose and about six inches away from it, then with an outward and backward sweep is brought at right angles to the body; it is then folded and drawn to the side ready for the next stroke.

The upper arm should pass the under arm whilst being lifted to its outward reach. The under arm should be finishing when the upper arm and the legs are just commencing.

If perfect time and rhythm is kept, this is the most graceful of all strokes.

It will be seen there are three distinct movements in the side stroke. To attain regularity in combining them the beginner should count—one, two, three—to himself as first the legs, then the right and the left arms come into action. The beginning of each fresh movement with another limb should not commence before the previous one has expended the force of its action.

Swim as level as you possibly can, merely allowing the tip of the uppermost shoulder to be visible above the surface.

If you splash the water with your hands, your legs are too low; if with your feet, they are too high.

The Over-arm Stroke

The Over-arm Stroke.

This is practically the same as the side stroke, with the exception that the upper arm is brought out of the water to save resistance, and the swimmer must endeavour to get as much reach as possible with the top arm, the palm of the hand being outwards, as this straightens the body.

CHAPTER VI

THE OVER-HAND STROKE

THIS is a very useful and easy style of swimming, but I must warn beginners that they should on no account seek to acquire it before they have a thorough knowledge of the

Over-hand Stroke.

side stroke. If they do attempt it, the penalty is loss of speed and a slovenly style.

The movements in which the ordinary side stroke differs

The Over-hand Stroke

from the over-hand are those of the left or upper arm and hand. The arm is carried into the air, and thus a lengthened reach is obtained above the surface. The head should lie as far as possible back in the water, whilst the body, legs, and feet should be in a straight line with and quite close to the surface. When the left arm has been carried forward, and stretched as far as possible from the surface, the arm and hand re-enter the water, and a strong propelling stroke is pulled through it. Don't swing the arm uselessly round from the shoulder, but carry it through the air quietly, yet gracefully.

The leg work is simultaneous with the left-arm movements. Thus they are drawn up when the left arm reaches forward, they are widely stretched when the arm is ready to pull, and they are pulled strongly together simultaneously with the strong movement of the uppermost arm.

Breathing should be regulated in precisely the same way as when the side stroke is employed.

CHAPTER VII

TOUCHING AND TURNING

THE term "touch and turn" was brought into vogue by reason of the many swimming races held throughout the country in comparatively small baths. It became the custom when races were first indulged in for competitors to push off with the feet, thereby gaining more or less of a good start, according to the strength of the impetus.

If the swimmer is using the side or over-hand stroke, and going on the right side, the left hand, when within three feet of the end wall of the bath, ceases its propelling movement, and reaches in front of the head until it touches the wall above water-mark. When the palm of the hand has been placed horizontally against the wall, the fingers should be turned to the right, being the direction in which the swimmer should turn.

The knees must now be bent, and the body, being close to the wall, turns on its own axis to the right, assisted in doing so by the left hand. Now the feet should be brought into play, and pressed firmly against the wall. This action brings the body, arms, and hands into a straight line, the head being between the biceps under water. Let the swimmer now double up his thighs under his loins, so that the calves of the legs touch the backs of the thighs, press his feet hard against the wall, push off with might and main, and he will find that he has made very good progress in the new length he is just about to negotiate.

CHAPTER VIII

TREADING WATER

POSSIBLY the most useful variation in ordinary swimming is that popularly known as " treading water."

There is no end, in fact, to its usefulness, even to an expert.

It is employed when a swimmer wishes to raise his head as high out of the water as possible, when he intends to divest himself of upper clothing, or if he wishes to grasp a bough or rope above his head. It also enables him to partake of refreshment when a long swim is in progress, is useful for the purposes of conversation, and is altogether a most easy method of progression.

Many people entertain the idea that " treading water " is an extremely difficult feat. As a matter of fact it is very easy.

It furthermore should be learnt by every one, as it is the only department of the art that is at all natural. In fact the attitude and action assumed are exactly those of walking upstairs.

There are three methods of treading, and the reader can please himself as to the one he selects. All are very practical and easy of acquirement.

The First Method.

The first and most common method is to extend the arms at right angles to the body. The palms must be down-

Treading Water ; a Saver of Life

wards—hold the head up, the chin just touching the water.
Keep the hands below water, and tread quickly as though
running upstairs. The body will then rise considerably out
of the water.

Second Method.

The second method is to place the hands on the hips, inflate the chest, and keep the head well up. Kick the legs
outward from the knees, first to the front and then to the
back. The body will move forward, but will at the same
time have a tendency to rise above the surface.

Third Method.

With the third method the arms are folded across the
chest. The legs are then drawn backwards alternately, and
this motion has a tendency to move the body in a backward
direction.

I should recommend every swimmer to learn all three
methods. By so doing he will be able to tread water in any
direction instantly should occasion require it.

Treading Water; a Saver of Life.

If every one only learned to tread water, three-fourths
of the deaths that occur from accidental immersion would
be prevented.

Suppose now a man who knew nothing whatever of swimming fell into water. The natural action would be for the
legs to sink and the body to assume a consequent perpendicular position. But the water splashes over the face, the
eyes, nose, and mouth become filled with it, the man is
immediately terrified at his unaccustomed and unexpected

Treading Water ; a Saver of Life

plight, and consequently he at once throws up his hands, and down he goes.

If those unable to swim at all would or could but remember at such a moment that on becoming submerged one should keep perfectly inactive for a brief time, all would be well.

The head will soon rise above the surface, and at that moment the hands should be alternately beaten downwards. At the same time the head should be held well back. This prevents the water from entering the eyes, nostrils, and mouth.

Now an effort should be made to work the legs in just such a manner as one employs when walking upstairs.

In this way at least many people totally unable to swim could easily keep afloat without sustaining a second immersion, until a rescue could be effected.

A treading competition is usually a most artistic affair, and those learning this branch would do well to witness one before attempting the same movements themselves.

Treading Water.

By doing so they will learn to avoid bobbing up and down, and to show as much of the body as possible above the surface.

CHAPTER IX

UNDER-WATER SWIMMING

THIS is a very useful accomplishment, and should be acquired by every swimmer. At the same time the ability to swim thus is woefully abused by many pot-hunters, and is to be deprecated, inasmuch as often permanent injury is done to the respiratory organs in an attempt to gain a prize.

Once under the water the swimmer should move in the usual way, or on the contrary, he may keep his hands stretched before him, thus enabling him to cut the water the more easily. At the same time such action greatly relieves his chest.

It is just as well that the novice, before he attempts under-water swimming, should have learned to open his eyes under water. This will enable him to ascertain at what depth he is immersed.

Remember that in under-water swimming in whatever direction the head is pointing the body will follow.

If a fairly long swim is to be attempted, the head should be kept as near the surface as is possible. This considerably reduces the pressure, and is a measure of wise precaution.

When symptoms of distressed breathing or suffocation are felt this precaution will be found to be invaluable, as a single effort will bring the swimmer's head above the surface, and much trouble and pain will thereby be avoided.

Do not forget, too, before starting to empty and thoroughly

refill the lungs, as I advise in another chapter on diving. This is always a good method of increasing one's staying powers.

An Important Word of Warning.

I cannot refrain from a very earnest word of warning at this juncture.

So great is the desire on the part of those who have learned to swim under water "to break records" that I have known many foolish fellows who have actually imperilled their lives even after their common sense must have warned them that it was high time to give up, by attempting still to remain below the surface.

In bath competitions, for this very reason, I have seen dozens of young men and boys brought out of the water absolutely unconscious, and in several cases where the competition has taken place in a river the would-be record-breakers have been drowned.

If when swimming under water a sharp pain strikes the back of the neck, give up at once.

Again, if no neck pain occurs, but the action of the legs and arms is heavy, immediately rise to the surface.

Especially should these warnings be observed when swimming under water in rivers or the sea. It is no reason that because Tom, Dick, or Harry can swim so many seconds or minutes under water you can do likewise.

Try by all means to acquire this accomplishment, but never attempt to go beyond your strength. Used discreetly, your powers of staying under water may be the means of saving life at some time or other, and even of saving your own should your legs become entangled in weeds or other obstruction.

CHAPTER X

SWIMMING LIKE A DOG

A GOOD mode of swimming, and a great relief when going a distance, is to emulate a dog's movements when in the water.

It is a very simple trick, and one which most swimmers can perform with comparative ease.

The name of this method explains itself, for each hand and foot is used alternately as a dog uses his feet when swimming.

The hands are alternately drawn down towards the chin in a compressed form and then expanded and slightly hollowed, with fingers closed.

As they strike the water the legs are kicked out straight to the rear. The sole of each foot should strike the water separately, the legs not working together as in the breast stroke.

This stroke, employed for a few minutes, affords a change of action, and relieves the strain on the muscles of both legs and arms when a mile or two has to be traversed.

If a dog's forepaws were tied together, and his hind legs also, he could still swim with the greatest ease. So it would be if a man were similarly served. For instructions how to perform a very effective and seemingly difficult feat, with both hands and feet securely bound, turn to the chapter on " Water Tricks " on p. 60.

CHAPTER XI

OVERCOMING DIFFICULTIES

The Cramp.

UNDOUBTEDLY this affection, to which all swimmers are liable, is a most unpleasant and dangerous experience. At the same time there is not so much danger in cramp as is generally supposed.

Losing presence of mind has undoubtedly been responsible for more deaths than the actual seizure.

Personally I have several times been caught by it when swimming in very deep water, but except for the pain, have never felt particularly inconvenienced.

When seized with cramp in any part, if the shore is handy lose no time in reaching it.

Remember that even should both legs be disabled you can paddle ashore with your hands. If both arms are seized, you have only to lie on your back and get to land by striking with your legs.

Should, however, assistance not be at hand, and the shore far away, different tactics must be adopted.

First of all, retain your presence of mind.

If the cramp is felt in the calf of the leg, just below the knee (the most usual place), turn on your back at once, bend the toes upward, kick out the affected leg in the air, ignore the pain, paddle with one hand, and with the other rub the spot smartly.

Bringing Things Ashore

Cramp in nearly all cases is due to indigestion, but in a few instances I have known it to have been brought about by the low temperature of the water. Again, there are many persons who are always seized with it after having been in the water a little time. These will do well never to go out of their depth.

Weed Entanglements.

Very often the clearest and cleanest looking stream contains a death-trap in the shape of weeds growing at a depth not noticeable to the swimmer but sufficiently near to entangle his legs.

Presence of mind, of course, is again here needed, directly progress is stayed.

The swimmer should at once lie as flat as he can, keeping the whole body and limbs as near to the surface as possible. Then with the feet a few rapid but very short strokes should be given, as at the same time with hollowed hands he pulls the water towards him. Even water-lilies, which are tough enough in all conscience, are broken easily by this treatment.

Bringing Things Ashore.

Suppose some object is met with in the water that is worth bringing ashore, the difficulty at once presents itself as to how it should be held so as at the same time to propel it and yourself to land.

This can be accomplished by swimming on the side and keeping the feet deeply sunk. The hand that is to grip the object is then raised out of the water, and having taken hold of whatever is to be secured, the other will be used to propel under water.

Encumbered by Clothes

Getting into a Boat.

It is one matter to dive from a boat into the water, but it is quite another to re-enter it successfully from that element even when assisted to do so; unless great care is exercised, the boat may even be upset by the struggles of the swimmer to get on board.

When it is desired to enter a boat from the water, swim to the stern, never to the sides. In gripping the boat keep the feet on the surface of the water, otherwise the legs will be sucked under the keel.

Gather yourself together for an effort. Then, with a vigorous kick and a jerk with the muscles of the arms, you find yourself rising from the water and lying on your breast over the stern. To crawl into the boat is an easy matter afterwards.

Another good method is to have an oar projecting over the stern or even a boat-hook in the same position. This can be grasped by the swimmer, and assists him greatly to re-enter the boat.

Where ladders of rope are available, they will prove of great assistance.

Encumbered by Clothes.

If you were out sculling by yourself, and the boat over-turned, a formidable obstacle to safety would be your clothes.

There is, of course, no great effort required to reach the shore, if only a short distance away, when so encumbered. But if the land be anything over fifty yards distant, clothes would be found unbearable and even dangerous to the swimmer's safety.

Encumbered by Clothes

The best method, therefore, is to rid yourself of them a once.

If you are wearing a coat, get rid of it. Tread water, divest yourself of the garment, and fling it as far from you as you possibly can.

Boots must next be shaken off. Lie on your back, bend either one of your legs, get the foot up as far as possible, and with one hand unfasten the lace or the buttons. Go through the same process with the other boot, and first with one toe and then with the other on the heel of the neighbouring boots prise them from the feet.

It is just as well to learn how to undress completely when in the water, so I will next show how the trousers may be taken off.

Lie on the back, give short little strokes with the feet, at the same time releasing braces or belt. Still working the feet, the trousers can be slipped as low as the knees. Then paddling with the hands, the feet can be shaken, and the garment will slip from the legs.

It is a good thing to practise for such emergencies.

I have often jumped into the water attired in an old lounge suit and swam until tired in the heavy dragging weight. Again, immediately I have entered the water so attired I have started to undress myself. At first, of course, I experienced considerable difficulty, but after a little practice I could divest myself of the garments with ease.

Excellent practice may be had, too, in swimming across a narrow stream with a small boy astride one's shoulders.

CHAPTER XII

PLUNGING AND DIVING

PLUNGING and diving are perhaps the finest amusements connected with swimming. "Low diving," "high diving," "deep diving," "headers," and "skimming plunges" are all worth learning. Certainly every swimmer should know at least how to plunge.

I can imagine no more clumsy way of entering the water, say, from a boat, than by jumping in feet foremost. Not only is it awkward, but in nine cases out of ten such a proceeding meets with a sharp blow against the chin, when it strikes the surface of the water.

It is just as easy to enter the water gracefully as clumsily. A little care only is required, but most beginners feel a sensation of alarm on their initial attempt to enter the water head first.

The "Header."

The "header" should be attempted as a preliminary.

The banks of a river, or that of a canal, are ideal places for this undertaking. The novice should stoop down until he is nearly double, put his hands together over his head, lean over until they nearly touch the surface, and then quietly and easily allow himself to fall into the water.

The first attempt is sure to be a failure, but the second will probably be a success. This is due to the fact that every one feels the sensation that his skull is likely to be fractured when the first plunge is taken. When the first essay has proved this idea to be false, the tyro turns his attention to the matter in hand and its successful accomplishment.

A method adopted with great success by many instructors is for two other swimmers to hold a towel before the diver, over which he plunges. If those holding the towel raise it as the dive is made, the legs of the learner are forced into a correct position, and the attempt is made easy.

The correct attitude for taking a "header" is to join the hands together over the head. This presents a wedge by which the water is separated for the passage of the head. If the hands are held loosely, it is very probable that the diver's head will be severely hurt when contact with the water is made.

The back should be well hollowed, the legs kept firm, with feet pressed tightly together, and the plunge should be made with a good deal of spirit.

A perfect "header" should raise no splash, and when the body has disappeared below the surface of the water, only a few rings and bubbles should be left to show the spot where the diver has vanished.

The High Dive.

High diving should next be essayed. Greater care is required, more especially if the water be shallow. The first time a novice leaps head-foremost even from a height of five feet, a most disagreeable sensation is experienced that much of the internal anatomy has been left behind on the bank. This is conquered and forgotten after one or two attempts.

The high dive may be termed a mere drop at a downward

The " Running Header "

angle, and is taken in a similar manner to the " header."
All learning the high dive should seek to become so proficient that if a wooden hoop be thrown into the water
beneath them, they can dive through it without touching
the sides.

The "Running Header."

Next the "running
header" may be tried.

A spring diving-board is
nearly always used for this
purpose. Mark off about a
twenty-five feet run, and
when the end of the board
is reached, jump ! The body
shoots out, and the impetus
given by the spring of the
board causes the body to
shoot high up into the air.
The body then becomes
straightened, the head declines towards the water,
which should be entered
without the slightest splash.

How to Dive.

Diving Feet First.

Curiously enough there
are some people who can
never learn to dive. This can only be attributed to the
fact that they never get over the initial " fractured skull
fear."

They, of course, aver that they prefer entering the water

53

Shallow Water Diving

feet first, and no doubt would be highly indignant with me if I omitted to detail how experts at diving feet first enter the water.

So I hasten to say that the body must be kept very erect as a preliminary, with the head slightly back. The arms must be placed firmly by the sides, and the breath held when the jump is made. If this is not done, the water will be forced up the nostrils in a most disagreeable manner. Don't open the legs until the water is entered. Then spread out both arms and legs, and the impetus gained by the jump will be considerably minimised.

If it is preferred, the arms may be raised over the head, the fingers being locked together, and the dive made in this manner. Indeed, when diving from a great height this is the safest method, as the arms serve to keep the body perpendicular.

Shallow Water Diving.

Leaping into shallow water, when the depth is not sufficient to permit of the ordinary plunge, is an invaluable accomplishment.

Take a run forward, then throw the body nearly, but not quite, horizontally into the water. Curve the back as far as possible when the head has touched the surface. Hold the body firmly braced, as any sudden change of curve in its attitude may add to disastrous results. In this manner even so shallow a depth as three feet may be successfully negotiated.

General Remarks.

Courage and presence of mind are all that is necessary to make an expert diver.

How to "Come up Again"

Many people believe, and some writers have stated, that it is impossible to open the eyes under water. This is absurd. It is as easy to open and shut the eyes when beneath the surface as it is to do so when above it.

The management of the breath is just as important as the sight. On making the first few attempts the novice is only able to remain under water a very short time—only a matter of seconds, in fact. By degrees, however, he will learn to retain his breath in quite an easy manner. The following hints will enable most people to remain beneath the surface for quite a long time after the first few attempts.

Before diving take a very full breath. Then expel every particle of air from the lungs. Repeat this several times slowly. Then enter the water, and it will be found that no difficulty is experienced in keeping beneath the surface for half a minute at least.

It is best not to tax the lungs too much at first ; by dint of constant practice gradually accustom them to longer periods of inaction.

How not to Dive.

How to "Come Up Again."

Reaching the surface can be accomplished in two ways. One is to remain perfectly still, and by so doing the body will rise like a cork. The other method, and by far the best, is to strike strongly downwards with the feet, as

55

in the act of leaping. At the same time raise the hands above the head, and the effect will be as if the diver is being pulled towards the surface. Indeed, the body will actually shoot out of the water until the whole of the waist is exposed.

CHAPTER XIII

TRAINING

No animal is so much improved by training as man. At the same time, whilst reading these remarks of mine on the subject, it must be distinctly understood that I recognise the fact that what agrees with one man, and makes him thoroughly fit, will well-nigh kill another.

I am basing this article on all-round observation. Pluck, I have found, does much, but training does a great deal more. It is impossible for a man to accomplish either a long or a short distance swim in good time without systematic training.

Speaking personally, I commence training in March. I then take long walks interspersed with swims three times a week. On Monday, say, I swim for three hours, on Wednesday four hours, and on Saturday six.

Cycling and swimming do not go well together, and on no account should short-distance men be votaries of the wheel.

Nobody under thirteen stone in weight should ever attempt long-distance swimming, and even then, unless plenty of time to train can be given by the swimmer, long attempts are best left alone. With long-distance swimming, too, success will greatly depend upon ability to resist the cold. Constitution is everything. Training can do much, but unless you have a constitution to work upon, do not attempt record-breaking of any description.

First of all, then, never eat just prior to a contest, nor for

Training

three hours before it. Smoke very little, if at all. Give up the use of alcohol gradually. Mild aperients taken twice a week do good; and only plain and digestible food should be eaten.

Nearly all amateur swimmers are engaged in business during the day, and they will find it a good plan to walk to their work, and to return home also on foot if the distance is reasonable. Their motto should be "Fresh Air for Ever," and they should see that they get plenty of it. Avoid late hours, and be out of bed by 6 a.m. A cold tub with a big sponge and lots of water, followed by a severe rubbing with a rough Turkish towel, ought to be the first item of every swimmer's daily programme.

Because your chums Tom, Dick, and Harry eat so much when training, it does not follow that you should do the same. Eat just what you require and know to be good for you, and no more.

At first long, steady swims should be indulged in every day. If, however, it is found by the individual that he is feeling "done up," the number of practises should be at once reduced to half. If your practice is being taken in a bath, *swim*—do not play about.

Keep your hair cut short, or colds may be caught. Practise in the same kind of costume that you intend to race in.

If you are training for a short speed contest, do not tire yourself with work on the day of the race. For your training take gentle walks, never neglect your morning tub, and in addition take light dumb-bell exercise, an occasional hundred yards sprint each day, and, of course, the usual water practice.

For contests that exceed a third of a mile in accomplish-

Training

ment, the swimmer should traverse quite double the distance at least twice a week before the race, and on one occasion, at least, the course should be covered at top speed.

If you are going to race in a town a hundred miles from your home, get the train ride over a day prior to the contest. You will thus not be deprived of your sleep and consequent rest.

Many young swimmers think that by constantly practising and spurting they improve their pace. The reverse is generally the case. Only a long course of *steady* practice and judicious training can ever accomplish such an end.

These rules, carefully observed, will be found practicable by most swimmers, but, as we have seen, no book ever written on the subject can possibly give a correct formula that may be adopted with success by everybody.

CHAPTER XIV

WATER TRICKS

To learn a few tricks for performance in the water is a diverting change, as very many of them are a source of amusement both to swimmer and spectator.

With the majority of tricks there are no great difficulties as a rule to be overcome. The would-be performer, however, should not attempt any "exhibition swimming," as it is commonly termed, until he is moderately proficient, or at least feels fairly at home in the water.

Porpoise Swimming.

This is a great favourite wherever shown, and may be rendered by one or by a dozen swimmers simultaneously. In the latter case the performers should dive and reappear together.

Clear the lungs well, first of all. Take in a full breath and let the body sink under the water just as the inspiration ceases. Under water, give a couple of breast strokes, turn the head upwards, then vigorously kick the legs. Just prior to the head coming above the surface give an ordinary arm stroke, and as the head pops above water execute the breast stroke, and force the arms downwards to the side of the hips. The body will then have rolled over like a porpoise.

The Spinning Top.

Turn on your back, double up the body by bringing up the knees to the chin, cross the legs, and "scull" with the hands. After a moment, push the water from your breast, as it were, with the right or the left hand, whichever you are most ready with. Then use the reverse hand to pull the water towards the body. After half a dozen such movements have been made it will be found that the body is spinning round and round in the water, just as a top would turn on the ground.

Tug of War.

Two swimmers place themselves horizontally on their backs. The legs should be strongly extended. Now let the feet lock within each other, and both swimmers pull backwards simultaneously with all their power. The one who succeeds in pulling the other back is, of course, the victor.

Wrestling.

Two swimmers place themselves in opposite positions. They then hold their right hands in the air and tread water. Now each places a hand on the head of his opponent, and try by pressure to force him under the water. Only the head of the adversary must be touched.

The Fugitive.

A good exhibition is that of a supposed manacled captive escaping across a river.

The hands and feet are tied together with handkerchiefs. Press the hands tightly together, with the fingers close to each other, and the whole hand made as flat as possible. Turn slightly on the left side, making the ordinary stroke with the legs, and bring the hands towards the left hip with a quick sweep, taking care to part them from it as soon as that

The Paddle-boat

movement is made. The feet, by reason of being tied, are
held together tightly at the ankles. Give short, sharp
strokes with them, the hands and feet working together.
Good progress across the water is made in this way, and
this being a very easy, though apparently very hard, feat to
perform, never fails to secure a long round of applause from
spectators. Professionals, indeed, term it the "gallery
trick" for this very reason.

The Paddle-boat.

Lay on the back, rapidly beat the water by alternate
blows of the feet, which should be pointed well. This beats
up a shower of spray like that from the paddle-wheels of a
steamboat, and propels the swimmer through the water at
great speed. By doing this it is possible for quite a novice
to race a fairly good swimmer for a short distance.

Marching.

Lay on the back in a floating position. Cross your arms
carelessly across your chest. Then propel your body feet
first by alternate actions of the legs, just as in walking.
When the foot is being drawn down, apply pressure. When
the leg is straightened, do it gently.

The Pendulum.

Float on the water with the arms stretched out in a line
with the body, but beyond the head. Throw the head well
back—keep the body perfectly still. Now take in a long
breath, and try to look at your feet. Draw the hands gently
towards the head until they touch the nape of the neck.
The body will now assume a perpendicular position. When

Smoking Under Water

this has been accomplished, bring the arms gently to the front of the body and extend them well outwards. Simultaneously the head must be sunk between the arms until the face and arms are lying on the surface of the water. This causes the feet to rise and the body to float on the surface face downwards.

To recover, incline the head slowly backward. Draw the hands again to the nape of the neck, and the feet will again sink, the body slowly taking a perpendicular position. As this comes about extend the arms well behind the head, keep the palms upward, gradually inclining the head back until the legs rise again. These movements repeated produce a swinging motion something like that of the pendulum of a clock.

Smoking Under Water

Smoke a cigar until it is well alight, then take up your stand on the diving board. Inflate the lungs, and just on the instant of diving rapidly thrust the lighted end of the cigar into the mouth. Use the breast stroke beneath the water, and whilst doing so blow gently *at* the cigar, care being taken on no account to draw inwards. This action causes the smoke to issue from the other end of the cigar and ascend to the surface of the water in curls. The smoke can be distinctly seen by the spectators, and " how it is done " excites much speculation.

Do not take more than a dozen strokes, after which quickly ascend to the surface, and as the head comes above water take the cigar from the mouth, care being, of course, observed that the lighted end does not get wet.

A moment later, to show that the cigar is really alight, swim as high in the water as possible and puff at it.

The Bosphorus Trick

This trick always obtains a great deal of applause, but much practice is required before perfection is reached.

The Bosphorus Trick.

The exhibition, variously known as the "Bosphorus Trick" and the "Monte Christo Sack Feat," is another good illusion.

Procure a sack large enough for you to move about in. At the bottom have some leaden plates securely fastened. At the top cut a hole large enough for a rope to pass through.

A great deal depends upon the assistant to make this trick a success, as I will now show.

The one who is to perform this feat must get into the sack with some show of hesitation. This will at once be taken advantage of by the assistant, who will use some force to make his principal submit to be tied up.

The latter, as soon as he enters the sack, takes hold of the double rope which he will find has been passed through the hole before mentioned to the inside. This he holds very firmly, whilst the assistant takes hold of the outside ends and ties them very tightly round the mouth of the sack. With very good effect two or three onlookers may be invited each to add a knot on their own account. But they might tie a thousand knots and it would make no difference, for the knots have only been made on the other side of the sack from that where the doubled rope passes through the hole.

When the fastening farce is complete, a tap from the assistant's foot warns the principal to inflate his lungs. Then he is hurled off the platform into the water beneath.

The leaden-loaded sack causes the diver to sink feet first.

The Torpedo

In this position he stays at the bottom of the bath for a few seconds, then releases the rope he is holding. The mouth of the sack is pushed open with both hands and the body emerges from its prison.

The Torpedo.

Turn on the back with the legs closed and quite straight. The hands, palms downward, should be moved in semicircles from left to right. This will cause the body to move slowly head foremost.

Very soon the palms should be turned upwards, and the hands brought just beyond the head. This action causes every part except feet and ankles to become submerged. Now swing the arms with a sweep from the body under the water, and you will find yourself making rapid progress feet foremost.

This is a difficult trick to learn, and if kept up too long is apt to overstrain the lungs.

Dinner Under Water.

Take a soft roll in the left hand, and whilst submerging the rest of the body keep that hand above the surface. Now rest one knee on the bottom of the bath, where the water is about four feet deep.

Fill the lungs well, then descend below the surface. With the right hand now break off a piece of the bread and carry it to the mouth. Exhale a little breath as the morsel is placed in the mouth. This prevents the water from entering.

The rest, or a greater portion, of the roll may be eaten in this way.

A Drink Under Water

A Drink Under Water.

Milk should be used, to show that there is no deception, and a small lemonade bottle should be half filled with this liquid, and well corked.

This should then be taken by the swimmer with him to the deepest end of the bath and uncorked with great care. Place the mouth of the bottle between the lips and pull the cork out sideways. Blow a little air out through the nostrils, and drink. When the swimmer feels he can swallow no more, he should at once recork the bottle, as if any of the milk escapes into the clear water, it looks as though he has poured the milk into the bath instead of having drank it.

This is a very difficult trick, and should not be attempted until the swimmer has been used to under-water work for a considerable time.

The Glide.

Two swimmers are necessary for this feat. They should place themselves on the surface of the water with the feet of one close to the head of the other. The first man now floats motionless. His legs should be closed, and his arms extended to beyond the head.

The second man now takes hold of the ankles of the other and pulls his feet towards his head. Then No. 2 ducks his head below the feet of his colleague, at the same moment pulling the other's legs over his body with all his force, loosening his grip of the ankles as he feels the body passing above him. The underneath swimmer carefully watches the body gliding above him, and as No. 1's head comes towards his

Somersaults Under Water

feet, No. 2's toes are skilfully inserted under the locked arms of No. 1.

Half a dozen people can act together in this feat with good effect, but when more than two are performing it must be done most mechanically, or the effect is spoiled.

Somersaults Under Water.

A forward somersault in the water is performed by pressing the head down upon the chest. The legs are drawn

Somersault under Water.

well up, and the arms brought in a straight line with the shoulders, at right angles with the body. The hands, palms downwards, are forced towards the front. This causes the body to revolve, as it were, on an imaginary axis, and in its own space.

A backward somersault is performed with the same movements reversed.

Double somersaults are performed by two swimmers. Both men must be experts at single somersaulting. The two swimmers must stand behind one another shoulder deep in the bath. No. 1 extends his arms at right angles,

Somersaults Under Water

and separates his feet until they are about twelve inches apart. No. 2 meanwhile inflates his lungs, dives, and places his head between No. 1's legs. No. 2 now bends his legs backwards until his feet come above water. No. 1 then places his head between No. 2's legs. When both swimmers feel each other's legs lightly gripping a head, No. 1 makes a movement of falling backwards. This is reciprocated by No. 2, and the locked bodies begin to revolve. The arm movement of the backward somersault is the means of propulsion, and as the heads of the swimmers alternately appear they should rise sufficiently above the surface to allow of ample breathing facilities. Not more than five successive somersaults should be indulged in.

There are, of course, many other so-called feats under water, but as the majority are so much trickery, and call for no ability whatever in performance, I do not propose to devote any space to describing them.

CHAPTER XV

SWIMMING ON THE BACK

I PROPOSE to devote considerable space to this particular item, because, on the one hand, it is my favourite method of progression, and on the other, the great importance of swimming on the back has not been recognised as it deserves by the majority of even expert swimmers.

It is not the fastest method of progression, I am well aware, but its value when long-distance swimming or life-saving is the object cannot be over-estimated.

Learning the Ordinary Back Stroke.

Walk into the water breast high, turn away from the shore, take a long breath, then lie gently backward in the water. Keep your hands on your waist and extend the elbows outward. Expand your chest, hold your breath.

Just at that moment when you lie back, very little exertion will lift the feet off the ground. As they rise spread your legs outward as far as possible. Your position in the water is like the letter Y, the legs, of course, constituting the branches of the letter.

Now bring your legs firmly and closely together. Turn your toes upward. Do not jerk the movement, and you will find the body is propelled forward. When the impetus thus gained is nearly expended, bend the legs so that the feet are drawn close up to the trunk. Knees should be outward, heels together.

The stroke is renewed by spreading apart, closing again, and so on.

The management of the breath should be particularly noted.

When spreading and closing the legs *inhale* breath. *Exhale* as the feet are drawn up to the body.

As practice makes perfect, greater speed may be acquired by using the hands as sculls. Carry them outward, but on a level with the body, palms downward. As the arms assume a horizontal position the wrists are turned, to allow of the palms of the hands facing towards the feet. Elbows, wrists, and hands are now firmly braced, and a strong pull towards the legs is made. This should be done as the legs are being closed.

A Second Back Stroke.

As a variant to this : Bend the elbows downward, allow the hands to be carried upwards along the sides of the body, palms downward. When the hands have been carried in this manner up to the armpits, pull strongly towards the legs, and a propelling movement is the result.

The Writer's Own Favourite Stroke.

A very powerful stroke, and a great favourite of mine, is to carry the hands up to the armpits, as described in the last method. I then turn the wrist so as to allow the palms of the hands to face outwards. My fingers then point in the direction in which I wish to progress. I now stretch both arms as far as possible in a line with the body and beyond the head, turn the wrists half round, thumbs upward, and sweep both hands outward and round until they touch the legs, and the arms are once more straight along the sides of the body.

This is not ornamental swimming, I must admit, but it has its compensating advantages in its power and speed.

Yet another Back Stroke.

A rather faster stroke is performed by lifting hands and arms out of the water at the finish of the pull downward, carrying them in the air, stretching them at full length forward beyond the head, and then dipping them into the water.

The kick is delivered to each stroke of the arms, the legs being drawn up as the arms are swung up in the air, and closed as the arms are pulled through the water.

Still another Way to Learn Back Stroke.

Another very good way to learn swimming on the back is to lie as in floating, and then gently to paddle with the hands, keeping the fingers firmly together the while, and scooping the water in the direction of the feet.

When the novice can do this fairly well he should next attempt scooping the water towards his head. The course can be steered by scooping more forcibly with one hand than with the other.

The legs should next be called into play, by striking them apart in the Y fashion already shown, and bringing them together firmly and strongly.

I know of no better illustration of how to swim well in this particular way than to watch the otters and seals in the

Zoo. They keep their forepaws close to their sides, there is no inelegant splashing of water, and the hinder paws are opened and shut with a steady sweep, the wedge-like mass of water between them when wide open being excluded with clockwork-like action.

The feet in back-swimming should always be kept about a foot below the surface; if they are kept too high the stroke is apt to drive the upper part of the head and eyes under the water.

Furthermore, the novice should always remember that it is simply impossible to arch the spine too much, or to press the head too far between the shoulders.

Steering.

Steering a course, too, may be managed by means of either arms or legs. Allow the left leg or arm to remain still, and use the right, and the body will as a result be driven to the left, and so in the reverse direction when the reverse means are employed.

Swimming on the Back, using Arms only.

Swimming on the back without employing the feet should also be learned, as this mode serves to strengthen the arms in an extraordinary degree without in the least fatiguing the breasts.

The body is placed horizontally, with the feet stiffly outstretched. The heels and toes are kept in contact. The body is somewhat curved and the hands are stretched flatly forward over the body, and moved slowly in small circles. As each stroke is made the hips are somewhat drawn up.

CHAPTER XVI

SEA SWIMMING

NOTHING, to my mind, is more delightful than " a dip in the briny." But I am well aware that to the average man or woman, who has learnt to swim in baths or fresh water, the change to breakers and waves from dead water is far from pleasant on the first encounter.

Nearly everybody attempts to breast or mount the waves. This is a great mistake, as by taking their direction the swimmer is unexpectedly carried a long distance.

Beginners Entering a Rough Sea.

Even in fairly calm weather the force of the breeze at the seaside is often sufficient to lift a man off his feet and throw him down at full length into the water. The succeeding breakers then have him at their mercy if he does not know how to combat them.

To those who are conversant with entering the water properly there is no danger in swimming even in very rough weather.

Watch very carefully the advancing wave. If it does not seem to rise above the level of the nose, lean forward, and give a jump upwards as it begins to rise. Keep the arms stretched out slightly in front of and almost at right angles to the body as you leap. Then the wave will pass under your feet without you feeling any of its force.

The Good Swimmer's Method

Should the wave, however, come on with a great roar and rush, like a mountain rising before you, spread your hands well forward, stoop down, and let the foaming mass pass completely over you.

No cracked craniums are the result of the encounter—merely an enjoyable ducking. Of course you will not attempt to inhale whilst the flood passes above you. It will be all over in a second, and when it has gone by, and you find yourself in comparatively shallow water, you can then breathe once again, and leap the succeeding waves.

These directions, bear in mind, are for those who cannot swim at all, or only very little.

The Good Swimmer's Method.

Good swimmers employ a different method.

Watching for the break of a big wave, the swimmer rushes into the sea, and is carried out from the shore by it as it recedes. He surmounts the smaller waves, and dives through the very large ones.

To return to the shore, the easiest plan is to keep on the crests of the waves as they roll landwards. When the feet touch the ground, the swimmer should immediately rush out so as to escape the force of the receding water.

Study the Tides.

Never venture out to sea when the tide is running out. It is not only dangerous, but the swimming is very unpleasant.

When the tide is coming in, even if the water be rough, the swimmer may safely venture out some distance, but no swimmer, however good, should ever venture very far unless accompanied by a boat. Local knowledge is always advisable if a long swim is intended.

A little paper calculation before setting out for a swim will save the sea swimmer much needless exertion, and greatly add to the enjoyment of his dip.

At nearly all seaside places tide-tables are sold at the stationers' and newspaper shops. Half an hour's study of one will give an invaluable knowledge of the tides and their "sets." The swimmer can thus map out his course to go against the tide on the outward journey, and rely on its aid for the return.

Choose a Spot to Start.

When starting out for a swim from a secluded nook, the spot should be first visited at low water. The rocks, stones, holes, mussel-beds, &c., can then be noted, and avoided when wading out is undertaken.

But secluded nooks, by reason of the fact that they are generally small bays, are often dangerous bathing-places. Strong currents gather not far away, and the swimmer is perhaps carried out to sea very rapidly and unexpectedly.

In such an emergency he should never lose courage. At once strike out strongly in a diagonal direction for some spot on shore. Never mind if it is half a mile from where your clothes are laying. Brace yourself up for a long, hard swim, and settle down to it at once with the regularity of a machine and the determination of a record-breaker.

Sea-water Worries.

Rocks are unpleasant acquaintances for the bare feet. A good look-out should be kept for them even in fairly deep water. To land on one, swim up, keeping the hands well down and the body and legs as high up as possible. Then carefully feel with the hands for a spot on which to place the feet. When found, take hold quickly and rise out of the water.

Jelly-fish are more annoying than dangerous. Some, however, sting one badly—others leave wide scarlet marks on the skin as a memento of their acquaintance. These blister. In the former case use a carbonate of soda solution for bathing the part. For the latter, cold lead-water is the best remedy.

Deafness often comes about by excessive sea swimming. Those afflicted in this manner should never swim without ear-plugs of some kind.

The best time for sea swimming is undoubtedly in August. Nobody should swim in the sea before June or after October, for the night frosts are about, and are dangerous to the health of a naked person. There are many men, of course, in residence around our coasts who indulge in a daily swim all the year round. But they have done so from infancy, and use is everything in such cases. The man living in a town, however, cannot take such a liberty with impunity. If he does,

Colds, at the very least, will be the result. Some people imagine colds cannot be caught at the seaside. This is an erroneous idea. To guard against a chill, directly the water is left, a vigorous rubbing down with a coarse towel should be indulged in. Then a short run up and down the beach will not only prove enjoyable, but will brace the system besides.

CHAPTER XVII

OUT-OF-WATER SWIMMING

THOSE who choose to do so may learn much of the theory of swimming in their own bedrooms.

A knowledge of the strokes may be obtained by what is alliteratively termed "parlour practice." Some say it accustoms the muscles to the special actions which they will be called upon to perform, and possibly from this standpoint, if from none other, this particular drill deserves attention, and to some extent justifies the old and often ridiculed advice, "Do not go into the water until you can swim."

It is furthermore inexpensive, no outlay being needed for apparatus. I cannot say I have taken kindly to the exercise myself, because lying across a bench or a chair is not a pleasant pastime for the stomach. In fact, I find it very exhausting.

Faddists who favour the idea, however, aver that if the drills hereinafter set out are thoroughly acquired, the novice will in every case take to the water like a duck, swimming right away. Candidly, I have never seen such a phenomenon, and—I don't believe it.

Attired in a jersey, trousers, and canvas shoes, the pupil must stand at "attention."

1. Place the hands on the hips. Raise the right leg up,

the heel to touch the knee of the left leg. Point
the toes downwards as far as possible.

2. Now straighten the right leg, without touching the
   ground, then bring it down easily one pace to the
   right.

3. Bring the right leg up smartly to the left. Drop the
   hands to " attention."

Repeat these three movements with the left leg.

The next exercise should be to combine the right and left
leg movements, and this is how it is done :—

1. Place the hands on the hips. Now raise the body on
   the balls of the feet, opening out the knees as far
   as possible. Then sink down until the thighs and
   calves just touch.

2. Spring lightly and cleanly from the position just
   acquired on to the left leg, extending the right a
   long pace away, without touching the floor.

3. Get to " attention " again by drawing the right foot
   smartly alongside the left.

Practise these exercises little and often.

The arm movements may now be taken :—

Get into position at " attention," and raise the hands in
front of the chest. Thumbs and forefingers should lightly
touch, the fingers should be closed. Elbows well to the
side. Now, ready !

1. Place the head well back, and shoot the hands up-

wards to their fullest extent. Keep the hands well together.

2. Separate the hands, bring them round at right angles to the shoulders. Turn the hands outwards. Then describe slowly a quarter-circle with each hand.

3. Draw the elbows to the side and bring back the hands and arms to the position assumed prior to No. 1.

CHAPTER XVIII

LIFE SAVING

LAND RESCUE DRILL.

MOST persons who are good breast and back stroke swimmers and have thoroughly mastered the land rescue drills, as taught by the Life Saving Society in its numerous classes, can, after a little practice, easily perform in the water the movements learnt on land. The learner must, however, remember that a knowledge of the land rescue drill only, is not sufficient to make one an efficient and certain rescuer; practice in the water, on the lines laid down in the drills, is absolutely essential.

The following drills, which have been adapted to the practice of two persons, one acting as the rescuer and the other as the drowning subject, have been taken by kind permission from the Handbook of Instructions published by the Life Saving Society, London, which grants awards of various degree, from elementary to a high standard of proficiency, for personal ability to render aid to those in danger of losing their life by drowning.

The best way to become acquainted with the details of instruction is to get a friend to read out the commands, go carefully through all the drills, and, after a few lessons, those wishing to learn will be prepared to enter the water and perform the rescue methods as directed in the land drills.

At the start the two persons will take up their position in a line with one another at "attention." The right-hand person will be known as No. 1, and the one on the left of

Land Rescue Drill

No. 1 as No. 2, and they will proceed with their practice as follows :—

First Movements.

At the command "Two Deep," No. 2 will take a pace to the rear with the left foot. Another pace to the right with the right foot will bring No. 2 to the back of No. 1.

On the word "Inwards Turn," No. 1 will "about turn" and face No. 2; at the same time as No. 1 is turning, No. 2 will take a short pace to the rear.

At the word "First Method, Ready," No. 2 steps up a short pace, and grasps No. 1 by the arms, just above the elbows. No. 1 at the same moment places the heel of his right foot in the hollow of his left.

When the word "One" is uttered, No. 2 pushes outwards with his right hand and draws inwards with his left until No. 1 has been turned to a right angle.

At the command "Two," No. 2 looses his grip, reverses his hands, and repeats the foregoing movement, so that No. 1's back is turned towards him.

When "Three" is uttered, No. 2 lets go his hold, passes his hands up to the face of No. 1, who lays his head slightly back and covers his ears with the palms of the hands. Then get to "attention."

Second Movements.

Again "Inwards Turn"; on the word "Second Method, Ready," No. 2 steps up a short pace. He then grasps No. 1 by the arms just above the elbows. The latter places the heel of his right foot in the hollow of his left.

At the command "One," No. 2 pushes outwards with his right hand and draws inwards with his left. This turns No. 1 completely round until he faces the front.

Given the word "Two," No. 2 turns his thumbs outward

F

Land Rescue Drill

and fingers inward, and lifts No. 1's arms outward from the body.

At "Three," No. 2 brings his elbows close in to his sides and extends the arms of No. 1 until they are at right angles. Attention.

Third Movements.

Again "Inwards turn"; on the word "Third Method, Ready," No. 2 steps up a pace and grasps No. 1 by the arms just above the elbows. No. 1 places the heel of his right foot in the hollow of his left.

At the word "One," No. 2 pushes outwards with his right hand, and draws outwards with his left until No. 1 has been turned completely round and faces the front.

When "Two" is given, No. 2 pushes his arms under those of No. 1 as far as he possibly can.

At the command "Three," No. 2 bends his arms upward, places both hands flat over No. 1's shoulder joints, and brings his arms at right angles to his body. Get to "attention."

Fourth Movements.

Again "Inwards turn"; on the word "Fourth Method, Ready," No. 1 stretches out both arms at full length. No. 2 steps up and places the other's hands on his shoulders and close to the neck, leaning well back the while.

At the word "One," No. 2 stretches out both arms and hands, palms downward, right past No. 1's shoulders in the first position of the breast stroke.

Given "Two," No. 2 carries his arms outward and round in the second position of the breast stroke.

When "Three" is uttered, No. 2 recovers his hands to the position of renewing the stroke. "Front," and "attention."

This, then, completes the land rescue drill.

All swimmers should, besides learning a rescue drill, know how to escape from the clutch of a drowning person.

Land Release Drill

LAND RELEASE DRILL.

First Movements.

Again "Inwards turn"; on the word "First Method, Ready," No. 2 raises his hands until they are level with his shoulders. No. 1 at the same moment grasps No. 2's wrists.

At the word "One," No. 2 takes a pace to the rear with the left foot, raising his elbows until the arms are extended above the level of his head.

At "Two," No. 2 brings his hands down until they are in line with his hips, working his wrists outwards against the thumbs of No. 1. This, followed by a smart jerk outwards, causes No. 1 to release his grip.

Second Movements.

"Second Method, Ready." No. 1 raises his arms and clasps No. 2 round the neck, interlacing his fingers at the back of the head.

Given the command "One," No. 2 places his right foot outside the left foot of No. 1. He also places his left hand in the small of the other's back.

At the word "Two," No. 2 bends over, raising his right arm, and takes the nose of No. 1 between his second and third fingers, resting the hand flat on the chin.

When "Three" is given, No. 2 pushes the head of No. 1 smartly away, causing him instantly to release his hold.

Third Movements.

"Third Method, Ready." No. 1 passes his arms over those of No. 2 and clasps his hands behind the back.

At the word "One," No. 2 places his left hand on the right

Land Release Drill

shoulder of No. 1, and brings his right arm over the left of the other man, placing his open hand on the chin.

Given "Two," No. 2 lifts his right knee and plants it in the abdomen of No. 1.

When "Three" is uttered, No. 2 suddenly pushes against No. 1's chin with the right hand, at the same time giving a push with his knee in No. 1's abdomen. This causes No. 1 instantly to release his grip.

When these exercises have been thoroughly mastered, and can be executed with smartness and ease on land, they should be frequently practised in the water. Perfection can only be attained by practice.

It is our bounden duty, if possible, to save life; but when one feels one's strength is all but gone and a drowning person clutches at one, there must be no hesitancy as to what to do. Self-preservation is the first law of nature. Therefore,

If Clutched Round the Neck,

take a full breath, place your hand flat over nose and mouth, so that the nose comes between second and third fingers. Pinch your opponent's nostrils. This causes him to open his mouth and, by aid of the firm push off as directed in the land drill, you will release his clutch. His mouth fills with water and you have him under control at once, and not only save yourself from being drowned, but you stand a chance of rescuing him.

If Gripped by the Wrists,

turn both arms quickly against the other's thumbs. Bring your arms at right angles to your body. This effects your release.

If Clutched Round Body and Arms,

breathe deeply. Pinch your opponent's nostrils as in No. 1, and place your knee on his chest. Then push your arm and

Land Release Drill

leg out simultaneously. This knocks all the breath out of the other, and sends him from you a sufficient distance to allow you to effect your own escape, or gives you time to make up your mind by what means you may rescue him.

Resuscitation.

First of all send, if possible, for a doctor. In the meantime try to restore respiration.

If no sign of life is apparent, lay the patient flat on the back, loosen the dress, and place a folded coat or pillow under the head and shoulder-blades.

Wipe the mouth and nostrils, draw the tongue forward. Proceed by the Silvester Method to induce artificial breathing. Grasp the arms of the patient below the elbows. Then draw steadily upwards full length above the head, and down again until they are in line with the rest of the body. Slowly repeat this movement at the rate of fifteen times a minute.

If there are a number of people at hand, prevent them from crowding round the patient.

Don't use rough treatment, and don't twist the limbs in any way.

When natural breathing has been restored, place hot-water bottles or hot bricks at the soles of the feet, on the stomach, and under the armpits. Friction should not be resorted to until the patient breathes unaided. Then, and not till then, friction may be commenced on the legs, and so upwards along the arms towards the body.

If possible wrap the patient in a blanket, and when the power of swallowing has returned administer a very small quantity of weak brandy and water, wine, or beef-tea. After that try to induce sleep.

If no doctor can be procured, and respiration is difficult to induce, the arm exercise as above should be continued for hours if necessary.

Land Release Drill

The American method of resuscitation invented by Dr. Howard is a good one, and is easily put into practice.

Place the improvised pillow under the back, so as to elevate the stomach.

Carry the arms beyond the head and cross the wrists.

Clean the mouth, draw out the tongue.

The operator kneels down over the patient, grasps the lower ribs, spreading his fingers well apart over the chest, the thumbs pressing inward, and is very careful not to press the thumbs into the pit of the stomach.

Then he leans forward and pushes upward until his face is nearly level with the patient. As the ribs are pushed upward he lifts his hands off the patient and springs back to a kneeling position.

These movements should be made at the rate of fifteen a minute.

The two methods I have given are the most simple and practical to learn, and if an apparently drowned man cannot be restored by the one or the other, then he must have been dead when taken from the water.

Action, in all cases, must be prompt and well directed; and to acquire such proficiency all swimmers should learn, mark, and inwardly digest the following printed instructions issued by the Royal National Lifeboat Institution and the Royal Humane Society, or take part in the classes held by the Life Saving Society.

I.

Send immediately for medical assistance, blankets, and dry clothing, but proceed to treat the patient *instantly* on the spot, in the open air, with the face downwards, whether on shore or afloat; exposing the face, neck, and chest to the wind, except in severe weather, and removing all tight clothing from the neck and chest, especially the braces.

Land Release Drill

The points to be aimed at are—first, and *immediately*, the RESTORATION OF BREATHING; and secondly, after breathing is restored, the PROMOTION OF WARMTH AND CIRCULATION.

The efforts to *Restore Breathing* must be commenced immediately and energetically, and persevered in for one or two hours, or until a medical man has pronounced that life is extinct. Efforts to promote *Warmth* and *Circulation*, beyond removing the wet clothes and drying the skin, must not be made until the first appearance of natural breathing; for if circulation of the blood be induced before breathing has recommenced, the restoration to life will be endangered.

II.—TO RESTORE BREATHING.

To Clear the Throat.—Place the patient on the floor or ground with the face downwards, and one of the arms under the forehead, in which position all fluids will more readily escape by the mouth, and the tongue itself will fall forward, leaving the entrance into the windpipe free. Assist this operation by wiping and cleansing the mouth.

If satisfactory breathing commences, use the treatment described below to promote Warmth. If there be only slight breathing—or no breathing—or if the breathing fails, then—

To Excite Breathing.—Turn the patient well and instantly on the side, supporting the head, and—

Inspiration.—Excite the nostrils with snuff, hartshorn, and smelling salts, or tickle the throat with a feather, &c., if they are at hand. Rub the chest and face warm, and dash cold water, or cold and hot water alternately, on them. If there be no success, lose not a moment, but instantly—

Land Release Drill

To Imitate Breathing.—Replace the patient on the face, raising and supporting the chest well on a folded coat or other article of dress.

Turn the body very gently on the side and a little beyond, and then briskly on the face, back again, repeating these measures cautiously, efficiently, and perseveringly, about fifteen times in the minute, or once every four or five seconds, occasionally varying the side.

[*By placing the patient on the chest, the weight of the body forces the air out ; when turned on the side, this pressure is removed, and air enters the chest.*]

On each occasion that the body is replaced on the face, make uniform but efficient pressure, with brisk movement, on the back between and below the shoulder-blades or bones on each side, removing the pressure immediately before turning the body on the side. During the whole of the operations let one person attend solely to the movements of the head, and of the arm placed under it.

[*The first measure increases the Expiration, the second commences Inspiration.*]

The result is *Respiration* or *Natural Breathing*—and if not too late, *Life.*

Whilst the above operations are being proceeded with, dry the hands and feet; and as soon as dry clothing or blankets can be procured, strip the body, and cover or gradually reclothe it, but taking care not to interfere with the efforts to restore breathing.

III.

Should these efforts not prove successful in the course of from two to five minutes, proceed to imitate breathing by Dr. Silvester's method, as follows :—

Land Release Drill

Place the patient on the back on a flat surface, inclined a little upwards from the feet; raise and support the head and shoulders on a small firm cushion or folded article of dress placed under the shoulder-blades.

Draw forward the patient's tongue, and keep it projecting beyond the lips: an elastic band over the tongue and under the chin will answer this purpose, or a piece of string or tape may be tied round them; or by raising the lower jaw, the teeth may be made to retain the tongue in that position. Remove all tight clothing from about the neck and chest, especially the braces.

To Imitate the Movements of Breathing.—Standing at the patient's head, grasp the arms just above the elbows, and draw the arms gently and steadily upwards above the head, and *keep them stretched* upwards for two seconds. [*By this means air is drawn into the lungs.*] Then turn down the patient's arms, and press them gently and firmly for two seconds against the sides of the chest. [*By this means air is pressed out of the lungs.*]

Repeat these measures alternately, deliberately, and perseveringly, about fifteen times in a minute, until a spontaneous effort to respire is perceived, immediately upon which cease to imitate the movements of breathing, and proceed to INDUCE CIRCULATION AND WARMTH.

IV.—TREATMENT AFTER NATURAL BREATHING HAS BEEN RESTORED.

To Promote Warmth and Circulation.—Commence rubbing the limbs upwards, with firm grasping pressure and energy, using handkerchiefs, flannels, &c. [*By this measure the blood is propelled along the veins towards the heart.*]

89

Land Release Drill

The friction must be continued under the blanket or over the dry clothing.

Promote the warmth of the body by the application of hot flannels, bottles, or bladders of hot water, heated bricks, &c., to the pit of the stomach, the arm-pits, between the thighs, and to the soles of the feet.

If the patient has been carried to a house after respiration has been restored, be careful to let the air play freely about the room.

On the restoration of life, a teaspoonful of warm water should be given; and then, if the power of swallowing have returned, small quantities of wine, warm brandy and water, or coffee should be administered. The patient should be kept in bed, and a disposition to sleep encouraged.

General Observations.

The above treatment should be persevered in for some hours, as it is an erroneous opinion that persons are irrecoverable because life does not soon make its appearance, persons having been restored after persevering for many hours.

Cautions.

Prevent unnecessary crowding of persons round the body, especially if in an apartment.

Avoid rough usage, and do not allow the body to remain on the back unless the tongue is secured.

Under no circumstances hold the body up by the feet.

On no account place the body in a warm bath unless under medical direction, and even then it should only be employed as a momentary excitant.

Land Release Drill

These directions are the result of extensive inquiries which were made by the Royal National Lifeboat Institution in 1863-4 amongst Medical Men, Medical Bodies, and Coroners throughout the United Kingdom. These directions have been extensively circulated by the Institution throughout the United Kingdom and in the Colonies. They are also in use in Her Majesty's Fleet; in the Coastguard Service; at all the Stations of the British Army at home and abroad; in the Lighthouses and Vessels of the Corporation of the Trinity House; the Metropolitan and Provincial Police Forces; the Metropolitan School Board Schools; and the St. John Ambulance Association.

The Lifeboat Institution also issue the following instructions for saving drowning persons by swimming to their relief:—

1st. When you approach a person drowning in the water, assure him, with a loud and firm voice, that he is safe.

2nd. Before jumping in to save him, divest yourself as far and as quickly as possible of all clothes—tear them off if necessary; but if there is not time loose, at all events, the foot of your drawers if they are tied, as if you do not do so they fill with water and drag you.

3rd. On swimming to a person in the sea, if he be struggling do not seize him then, but keep off for a few seconds till he gets quiet, for it is sheer madness to take hold of a man when he is struggling in the water, and if you do you run a great risk.

4th. Then get close to him and take fast hold of the hair of his head, turn him as quickly as possible on to his back, give him a sudden pull and this will cause him to float; then throw yourself on your back also and swim for the shore, both hands having hold of his hair, you on your back, and he also on his, and of course his back to your stomach. In this way you will get sooner and safer ashore than by any other means, and you can easily thus swim with two or three persons. The writer has even, as an experiment, done it with four, and gone with them forty or fifty yards in the sea. One great advantage of this method is that it enables you to keep your head up, and also to hold the person's head up you are trying to save. It is of primary importance that you take fast hold of the hair, and throw both the person and yourself on your backs. After many experiments it is usually found preferable to all other methods. You can, in this manner, float nearly as long as you please, or until a boat or other help can be obtained.

5th. It is believed there is no such thing as a death-*grasp*, at least it is very unusual to witness it. As soon as a drowning man begins to get feeble and to lose his recollection, he gradually slackens his hold until he quits it altogether. No apprehension need therefore be felt on that head when attempting to rescue a drowning person.

6th. After a person has sunk to the bottom, if the water be smooth, the exact position where the body lies may be known by the air-bubbles, which will occasionally rise to the surface, allowance being of course made for the motion of the water, if in a tide-way or stream, which will have carried the bubbles out of a perpendicular course in rising to the surface. A body may be often regained from the bottom, before too late for recovery, by diving for it in the direction indicated by these bubbles.

7th. On rescuing a person by diving to the bottom, the hair of the head should be seized by one hand only, and the

other used in conjunction with the feet, in raising yourself
and the drowning person to the surface.

8th. If in the sea, it may sometimes be a great error to
try to get to land. If there be a strong "outsetting" tide,
and you are swimming either by yourself, or having hold
of a person who cannot swim, then get on to your back and
float till help comes. Many a man exhausts himself by
stemming the billows for the shore on a back-going tide
and sinks in the effort, when, if he floated, a boat or other
aid might have been obtained.

9th. These instructions apply alike to all circumstances,
whether as regards the roughest sea or smooth water.

The Royal Humane Society issues almost the same
instructions, and adds these further hints :—

A Warm Bath.—In all cases of prolonged immersion
in cold water, when the breathing continues, a warm bath
should be employed to restore the temperature.

If from Intense Cold.

Rub the body with snow, ice, or cold water. Restore
warmth by slow degrees. It is highly dangerous to apply
heat too early.

Avoid bathing within two hours after a meal.

Avoid bathing when exhausted from fatigue or from any
other cause.

Avoid bathing when the body is cooling after per-
spiration.

Avoid bathing altogether in the open air if, after having
been a short time in the water, there is a sense of chilliness
with numbness of the hands and feet ; but—

Land Release Drill

Bathe when the body is warm, provided no time is lost in getting into the water.

Avoid chilling the body by sitting or standing *undressed* on the banks or in boats after having been in the water.

Avoid remaining too long in the water—leave the water immediately there is the slightest feeling of chilliness.

The vigorous and strong may bathe early in the morning on an empty stomach.

The young, and those who are weak, had better bathe two or three hours after a meal—the best time for such is from two to three hours after breakfast.

Those who are subject to attacks of giddiness or faintness, and those who suffer from palpitation and other sense of discomfort at the heart, should not bathe without first consulting their medical adviser.

To Persons who cannot Swim.

If you get into water beyond your depth, do not plunge, struggle, or throw your hands and arms out of the water. *Tread Water* in the erect position by moving the feet up and down, at the same time paddling with the hands, keeping them under water. If any person approaches to rescue you, preserve your presence of mind, and do not grasp him; do what he tells you. If any small object be thrown to you, place it under your chest or armpits, and do not struggle to raise yourself out of the water; your head will not go under if you follow these instructions.

CHAPTER XIX

SWIMMING IN OTHER LANDS

Germany.

THE German method of teaching swimming is certainly unique. Not only is it a very thorough, but it is a very rapid system too.

The apparatus used in schools in the Fatherland is a hempen girdle and a rope of five fathoms length. A pole eight feet long and a horizontal rail are fixed on a platform above the water, and there the teacher takes up his position.

The depth of water in a German bath is a uniform eight feet. The pupil is garbed in peculiarly constructed drawers, fastened by a waist-band.

First he is placed with his hands resting upon the horizontal platform rail. As he stands in this position, the teacher instructs him as to the movements of the legs when he enters the water. This is done by guiding the motion of one leg whilst the pupil sustains his body with the other.

When these movements have been gone through to the teacher's satisfaction, the swimming-girdle is placed under the pupil's arms. The teacher then takes the rope, and fastens one end to a ring at the back of the girdle. Holding the other end in his hand, he commands his pupil to leap into the water, and such is the strictness of military rule in

Germany, this order is always obeyed without the slightest hesitation. As the novice's head comes above water, the instructor at once, in a steady, firm voice, directs him to breathe out through the nose. Then the beginner is hauled out, and the feat repeated several times.

The rope is next run through a pulley block at the end of the pole, and attached to the young swimmer's girdle. The instructor holds the end of the rope, and tells the pupil to extend his arms stiffly forward, clasp his hands, stretch his legs stiffly out, with heels together and toes turned out and drawn up. The movements of the legs are then taught.

At the command "One," the legs are slowly drawn under the body. The knees are separated as widely as possible, and the spine is bent downwards. "Two"—the legs are stiffly stretched out quickly. The heels are separated and the legs describe the widest possible angle. "Three"—the legs, with the knees held stiffly, are quickly brought together, which lets the pupil recover his original position.

By degrees the commands "Two" and "Three" are uttered in quick succession, and the pupil must accelerate his movements accordingly.

Frequently, by this method of training, he is able to propel himself through the water at the first lesson.

The motion of the hands is next taught. At the command "One," the hands, held with palms together, are opened, and the arms are extended at an acute angle. The elbows are bent, the hands being brought up to the chin. "Two" —the arms are quickly stretched forward and the horizontal position regained. Whilst the hand motions are being learned the legs remain stiffly extended.

The arm and leg strokes are next practised together, and very shortly the tutor slackens the rope. When, and not before, the pupil can make fifty successive strokes, he is released from the rope, but the teacher is always within reach with his pole until the pupil can accomplish 150 strokes in succession.

France.

Bernardi's system of upright swimming is taught almost universally throughout France. This form is distinguished from other methods by reason that the swimming is conducted throughout in an upright position.

The pupil is first taught to float in an upright position. He is next taught to use his arms and legs whilst balancing his body in the water, and then to imitate the movements he would make with his limbs whilst walking on dry land. The movements of the head next claim a goodly share of attention. Then the pupil is told to stretch his arms laterally on each side, to move one foot forward and the other backward, always to float easily but progress slowly. A circular sweep of the hands and the action of the legs are next practised, together with a downward and forward movement of the feet.

This system of swimming is an invaluable one from a military point of view, and is probably the least fatiguing in vogue. All French soldiers are taught these methods, and in consequence can cross rivers and other streams very heavily accoutred.

Canada.

Undoubtedly the system that prevails in Canada was borrowed from the North American Indians. The side stroke is more generally employed, with a most peculiar modification. The swimmer starts upon his right side, and sweeps his right hand through the water, or rather thrusts it forward. This is followed by the left arm being swung just above the surface with a bold sweep, the hand dipping into the water when the arm is stretched out as far as it can reach. The body then turns over to the left side, when the arm movements are reversed, the left sweeping under the body, while the right swings forward and over.

This is undoubtedly a very fast method of progress, but it is so tiring that only the strongest of swimmers can keep up the movements for any length of time.

South America.

The swimmer lies horizontally upon his waist. The common motions of swimming are made at first. Then one arm is stretched forwards, as in the side stroke, but the swimmer retains his body position. The opposite hand makes a widely-described circle towards the hips. When the arm has completed this movement it is lifted from the water and thrust forward, stretched to its utmost length, then sunk with the hand flat into the water. The other hand is stretched as widely as possible, and a small circle described with it in order to sustain the body. As the large circles are described the feet make the usual movements. Considerable practice is required to perfect this system, but it is undoubtedly the fastest swimming known for short distances.

CHAPTER XX

LONG-DISTANCE SWIMMERS AND THEIR FEATS

Lord Byron's Long-Distance Swim.

In 1810 Lord Byron demonstrated that an ordinary swimmer could traverse the Hellespont. The actual breadth is barely a mile, but the distance covered by Lord Byron was about four miles, owing to the cross-currents.

Dr. Bedale's Enjoyment.

Dr. Bedale, of Manchester, once swam from Liverpool to Runcorn, and on another occasion from Bangor to Beaumaris, and up the Menai Straits. The Doctor was frequently seen floating in the river Mersey, having attached to his body a light mast and sail secured in a belt, by means of which he enjoyed himself for hours. The swim from Liverpool to Runcorn took place in 1837.

J. B. Johnson's Seven-Mile Swim.

J. B. Johnson was known as the " hero of London Bridge," a title he earned by diving from London Bridge to rescue a passenger who fell into the river from a steamer. This feat created considerable interest. In 1872 he announced his intention of attempting to swim the Channel, but little interest was taken in the matter. He did attempt the task, however, from Dover to Calais, but was prevented by the cold. He is said to have swum seven miles in about 65 minutes. The longest and most famous swim in early days was that under the auspices of the old London Swimming Club, the stipulations being that the competitor who could complete the greatest distance in the Thames without assistance or refreshment should win the championship and a gold medal. Fifteen of the leading swimmers of the day started from Teddington Lock; only two reached Barnes, the winner being Wood, who completed 8¼ miles, with the tide, in 3 hr. 16 min.

Boyton's Channel Swim-Sail.

Captain Boyton, after several attempts, successfully swam across the Channel in a patent dress, inflated with air. Captain Boyton's feat, although claimed to be an important incident in the world of swimming, deserves no position whatever in its records, owing to the fact that the Channel was navigated by Boyton with a paddle in his hands and a sail fixed to his feet.

Webb's First Attempt.

Considerable interest was aroused in the early part of August, 1875, when the statement became public that Captain Webb intended to attempt the remarkable feat of swimming across the English Channel.

His first attempt to accomplish this long-distance swim resulted in failure. This trial took place on August 12, 1875, and after swimming for 6 hr. 48 min. 30 sec., during which period he had covered 13½ miles, Webb was compelled to leave the water owing to his having been drifted 9¾ miles to the eastward of his course by the north-east stream and stress of weather.

Webb started 2 hr. 25 min. before high water at Dover on a tide rising 13 ft. 7 in. at that port. When he gave up no estimate could be formed as to the probable distance he would have gone west on it.

His Second Trial.

In his second and successful trial Webb started 3¼ hours before high water at Dover on a 15 ft. 10 in. tide, which gave him one hour and three-quarters of the south-west stream.

His point of landing is 21½ miles from Dover, as the crow flies, but the actual length of the swim was 39½ miles.

Very little rest was taken by Webb—in fact, hardly any. When he did stop it was to take refreshment, and then he was treading water. During the whole of the time he had no recourse to artificial aid in any way. Of this there is indisputable proof, for the journalists who accompanied him across were most careful in their observations, and were men whose accuracy could be absolutely relied upon. The temperature of the water was about 65 degrees, and the most extraordinary part of the feat was the fact that Webb never complained of cold.

For the first 15 hours the weather was splendid. The sea was as smooth as glass, the sun obscured during the day by a haze, so that the heat did not affect his head, and in the night a three-quartered moon lighted him on his way. The worst time began at 3 a.m. on August 25th, as then drowsiness had to be overcome and rough water was entered. At this hour he was only some 4½ miles off Cape Grisnez, and

Miss Beckwith's Long Swim

although he was not then strong enough to strike out a direct course athwart the new north-east stream for land, he was fetching well in for Sangette, where he would have undoubtedly have landed between 7 and 8 a.m. had adverse weather not set in. He finally landed on Calais sands after having been in the water 21 hr. 45 min.

Cavill's Alleged Success.

Considerable doubt was thrown upon the statement that Cavill accomplished in August, 1877, the task which Webb so successfully brought off. It seems a great pity that some steps were not taken to establish this record beyond all doubt, because if Cavill did swim the Channel it is greatly to be regretted that he did not—and remember, he easily could—have his arrangements so perfected that the feat could have been properly verified as Captain Webb's was.

Miss Beckwith's Long Swim.

On September 1, 1875, Miss Agnes Beckwith, then only fourteen years of age, swam from London Bridge to Greenwich, a distance of five miles, for a wager of £100. Commencing her journey at eight minutes to five with a steady breast stroke, Miss Beckwith covered the first mile and a half in 18 minutes. Limehouse Church—a trifle over half-way—was passed in 33 minutes, and Greenwich Pier was reached in 1 hr. 7 min. 45 sec.

Miss Parker's Record.

On September 4, 1875, Miss Emily Parker, who had previously undertaken to swim the same distance as Miss

Beckwith for a wager of £50 to £30, and who although only a few months older was much more robust, not only equalled but excelled the performance of Miss Beckwith. She went on to Blackwall, a distance of seven miles, finished, as she declared, "quite well and able to do a dozen miles further." Time, 1 hr. 37 min.

Dalton's Attempt.

On August 17, 1890, Professor Dalton left Folkestone for Boulogne with the intention of swimming across the Channel back to Folkestone, a distance of 27 miles. Dalton expressed his conviction that he could perform the journey in 20 hours, and so beat the time of Captain Webb. He entered the water at four o'clock on the Sunday afternoon, and accomplished the journey, it is stated, without any remarkable incident, at half-past three the following afternoon. At the bathing establishment he was attended by a doctor, being then in a state of collapse.

Holmes' Channel Swim.

Mr. Frank Holmes tried to swim the Channel from the English side on September 12, 1902. He entered the water at 6.30 a.m. near the Admiralty Pier, Dover, and struck out for the French coast; the conditions of water and weather alike were entirely favourable. The sea was smooth, the temperature of the water was exactly suited to the swimmer, and there was an almost entire absence of wind. Within two hours, however, the weather had become dirty, and Holmes had to face broken seas, which made his task impossible. He started with a breast stroke of

28 to the minute, and with four hours of the flood tide to run made rapid headway. When he had been at his task nearly two hours he adopted the side stroke. He was then nearly four miles out, and swimming strongly and well. Then with scarcely a warning a heavy squall swept down, and big waves broke right over the swimmer. Holmes kept the water until nearly nine o'clock, but at last reluctantly abandoned the attempt.

Holbein's Cross-Channel Swims.

About my own attempts at long-distance swimming the least said by me the better. I think, however, I may be pardoned for quoting and abridging a report by the London *Daily Express* of my cross-Channel swim on August 1, 1902, and also from the *Sportsman* of the August 27, 1902, attempt, respectively, without comment:—

From the " Daily Express," August 2nd.

Cape Grisnez, that desolate rock which exists for the purpose of maintaining one of the best lights in the world, looked big and bold in the sunshine as Mr. Holbein's tug dropped anchor on Thursday afternoon. The entire population turned out to welcome the swimmer.

From the very first the tides upset the calculations of the swimmer. In the choppy straits of Dover they swirl round and round in circles, and although the distance from shore to shore, as the gull flies, is only 18½ miles, no swimmer can hope to cross it with the most favourable conditions under a swim of 40 miles.

Mr. Holbein had consulted Captain Dane, commodore of the cross-Channel fleet, and other authorities, and his scheme was to take a north-north-westerly course, starting with a long leg to eastward on the flood, coming back westward with the turn of the tide, and being carried in to shore with the second easterly flood.

The experts said the best time to start would be from six to half-past. At five o'clock, while the tide was churning in over the snags of rock at the foot of Grisnez, the skipper of the tug altered all that, and told Mr. Holbein he must start at once. He was immediately prepared for the water. Over his body was smeared a thick treacly preparation of oil to protect him from the cold, and to save his eyes a linen mask, with mica goggles, was affixed with collodion to his face.

The French folk gave him a hearty cheer as he slipped off the rock and turned over for his back stroke. This is a stroke of his own invention, and very attractive and useful it is—a strong kick of the legs, and at the same time a complete circle with the hands from above the head to the thighs. He uses his arms like oars, and feathers the water carefully during his recovery. It is no stroke for a sprinter, but it is admirably adapted for long-distance work.

As Mr. Holbein came abreast the tug was got under way. The engines were uncoupled, and only one paddle was used, so that the swimmer, travelling on the lee side of the boat, was protected from the wind and swell.

" How do you feel? " shouted somebody from deck.

" Jolly," replied the swimmer; " but you ought to have started me sooner. I've missed an hour of the tide."

Everybody aboard was confident. The sea was still and smooth, and a light haze on the horizon showed that there was no wind in the neighbourhood. The temperature of the water was 63 degrees. A friend who went into the water for half an hour came out shivering, and clamouring for hot drinks, but Mr. Holbein, kept warm by his grease paints and his abnormally thick skin, was quite happy, working away at a steady 20 strokes a minute.

The South Foreland lights were picked up soon after dusk, for it was a clear night. But they looked very far away. At midnight the Calais boat went racing by, her searchlight shooting into the sky. The stars came out in their splendour, and a deep quiet enfolded the sea.

The people on the tug gathered astern, gazing with rapt fascination on the brown floating man with the masked face, swimming at his steady 20 strokes a minute. He was so cheery and well that Dr. Murphy left the tossing boat, and went aboard the tug for a nap.

But, swim as he might, Calais came distressingly nearer. The skipper calculated that he was not more than five miles from the coast. Slack tide was the only thing to pray for, and when it came Holbein made good progress—so good that by 1.30 one could see the riding lights of the ships anchored in the Downs.

The tide swung to the west, and the dim light of Dover could be seen. A great deal depended on that tide. To make the swim a success it had to carry the man on the inside of the Varne Buoy, which is 6½ miles from Dover, so that the angle might be right for the returning flood to take him ashore. The sky flushed with rosepink and yellow, and the sun came up. It revealed the discouraging fact that the French cliffs were considerably nearer than the English.

At five there was a consultation in the cabin, and the reckonings were marked on the chart. The result was bad. The course was running almost parallel with the

Holbein's Cross-Channel Swim

French coast, and to get inside the buoy was impossible. There was nothing for it but to persuade Mr. Holbein to save himself for another attempt.

" All right," said the swimmer, after a long pause, "but it's very hard lines. There has been some bad judgment somewhere."

Holbein refused the help of ropes or stretchers, and climbed first into the boat and then into the tug without assistance. He came out at six o'clock, after 12 hours and 20 minutes in the water, and was a good deal more concerned about the failure than about his own comfort. His temperature was 97½—only half a degree below the normal. His pulse was 94, against a normal of 72.

Holbein was cheered as he landed. During the swim he was fed every half-hour. He consumed three quarts of milk food—milk and Virol—a quart of cocoa, a drink of tea, a quantity of Bovril, and six raw eggs.

From " The Sportsman," August 29, 1902.

To his many brilliant performances, Montagu Holbein has added one of staying nearly 22½ hours in the water. This was in an attempt to cross the Channel, and, incidentally, beat the record of 21 hr. 45 min. made by the late Captain Webb as far back as 1875. Said record is the only accepted one for the cross-Channel swim, but there have been many aspirants for fame in this respect, notable amongst them being Frank Holmes, Montagu Holbein, and Madame Isacescu—all of whom were, curiously enough, present at Dover this week.

Holbein is a man of such pluck and determination that any advice of retreat to him is impossible, and though doubt was expressed for hours, there were hopes of landing him near the harbour extension works at Dover, and he was allowed to go on. At last, however, it became evident to even his most enthusiastic friends that prompt measures must be taken, and he was pulled out with much difficulty and against his will. His long stay in the water will certainly rank as one of the greatest in the history of swimming.

After being carefully rubbed with oils and a mask of American plaster fixed on his face with collodion, Holbein was taken ashore, and at 3.15 p.m. the start was made, Percy Nix having a short swim with him at the commencement. The course was made north-north-west, and the swimmer, using a back stroke at the rate of 20 a minute, made rapid progress. At 3.50 the old Cantab, R. G. F. Cohen, had half an hour's swim with Holbein, and hardly had he entered the water than the *La Marguerite*, crowded with passengers, came within hail. There was a scene of wild enthusiasm on board, and Holbein was delighted by the ovation they gave him. "That will encourage me to get across; in fact, I must get across after that," was his cheery remark, and they turned to their course and wished us goodbye.

At the expiration of the second hour's swim Holbein was four miles from the nearest point on the French coast and six miles from Cape Grisnez. Up to this point Holbein had been steered by discs placed in a boat, but he discarded them after the second hour and came alongside the tug. The improvement in the steering was quickly noticeable, and proved of great benefit to Holbein. Cape Blancnez was right astern when he had been in the water three hours, and the temperature was 64 degrees. At seven o'clock Grisnez

Holbein's Cross-Channel Swim

Light became visible to the south-west, the swimmer then being east of Blancnez, which was six and a half to seven miles away. The Calais Light flashed over the waters a few seconds later, and throughout the long night their sweeping flashes were constantly guiding our course. After four hours' swimming the South Foreland was to the north-west and Calais south-east, the French Harbour then being about seven miles off.

At ten o'clock it was estimated that we were 15 miles from Grisnez, 10 from the nearest point on the French coast, and 11 from the South Foreland. He was going wonderfully well, but the temperature of the water had, however, dropped to 61½. A big liner passed us going up Channel at 11 p.m., and at 11.50 the skipper thought Holbein might actually get in on the first western tide. The rising of the moon was a magnificent spectacle, and pleased Holbein, who up to this time had been lighted on his way by the Salsburg Flario Lights, which proved of excellent service. Soon after we lighted a flare on the bridge and tootled the syren in courtesy to the fast approaching mail boat for Calais. She put her searchlight on us, and under its piercing gaze Holbein looked weird and almost ghastly in the dark waters of the Channel. His stroke was strong and powerful, and he was as cheery as possible.

After one o'clock Holbein had a bad time, and was frequently vomiting. He kept asking about the Varne Buoy, which he had to get inside on the western tide, but the confidence of his attendants reassured him, and when asked how he felt, said, "Ten years younger since I started." After being in the water 12 hours he was again sick, but kept very confident. This was his worst time, but with the dawn he recovered a good deal. Soon after sunrise, which was a magnificent one, the Varne Buoy was west by south, and we were going north-north-west. Simons, of the Dover Club, was in with the swimmer, and was quietly pacing him. It was hazy round Dover, and the coast could hardly be discerned. Holbein was cheery, and talking quite freely.

Holbein, who had now been in about 19 hours, was repeatedly asking questions as to his course, and seemed rather worried about the distance of the nearest cliffs. At noon we were opposite St. Margaret's, when Holbein again questioned his guides. His voice was now much weaker, and it was evident that he was getting very tired. He had been in the water 21 hours, but was nearly two miles from land, and certainly four miles from the nearest spot he could get ashore on the tide. Asked if he was going to give it up, he said, "No, I shall keep on," and struggled gamely to reach the shore. But his strokes became weaker and weaker, while his voice betrayed the fact that he was suffering intense agony from the constant pour of salt water into his mouth. A hurried consultation between Messrs. May, Shorland, Bailey, Sinclair, and Watson ended in an immediate order for the swimmer to be pulled out. Such a marvellous Channel swim has never before been accomplished, and the only regret is that Holbein was unable to touch English soil before leaving the water. Everybody on board was sorry that he had to be lifted out, but as he was drifting away from the shore, there was no help for it.

CHAPTER XXI

HOW I TRAIN FOR A CROSS-CHANNEL SWIM

As any one who knows anything about swimming can imagine, the amount of preliminary work I have to go through before I attempt to negotiate the Straits of Dover is considerable.

Many people imagine that such an attempt is only a case of strolling down to the beach, undressing, wading out into deep water, and then making a bee-line for the opposite shore. As a matter of fact, for quite three months before I undertake a long-distance sea-swim I go into strict training.

It must not be thought by this remark that I attempt to get rid of flesh. On the contrary, I cultivate it if possible. The greatest obstacle in a long sea-swim which one has to contend with is cold. In addition to having the body well covered with flesh, one has to have the muscular system in good condition.

There are many splendid swimmers of my acquaintance who could not stand anything like the temperature I can swim in for hours at a stretch. This is my particular good fortune, of course, but it is my candid and honest opinion that no matter how good a swimmer a man may be, unless he possess that one qualification before all others, it will be utterly useless for him to attempt to cross the "waste of waters" 'twixt Calais and Dover.

To give an instance of the excessive temperature I can

swim in, I may place it on record that water heated to 125 degrees causes me no inconvenience. This would raise blisters on many men.

As I have remarked elsewhere, different methods of training have to be adopted by different people. Personally, the only change I make in my dietary is that I eat less vegetable food than I should otherwise. Twice a week I take a six-mile walk, and indulge in a seven hours' swim on every third day. On the days when neither walking nor swimming are to be found in my "Time Table" I take half an hour's exercise with a Sandow developer.

I feed well right up to the day of the attempt, and during my effort, whatever the length and time of it may be, I take constant nourishment—in fact, at half-hour intervals. No swimmer should feel that he is in need of food.

I have found that hot milk, raw eggs, hot tea, and Bovril are refreshing and staying foods. I take spirits only under very exceptional circumstances. Thus when "the last lap," so to speak, has arrived, I take some over-proof brandy beaten up with a new-laid egg. This enables one to spurt with increased vigour, but only just long enough to finish.

I never smoke, as I have always found it to be injurious to my staying power, and I seldom drink alcohol, as I regard spirits as being harmful to the constitution, even if taken moderately.

The next difficulty long-distance sea-swimmers always have to overcome is the action of the salt water upon the eyes. This temporarily blinds many swimmers, and unfortunately I am one of them.

As an instance of this, during my attempt to cross the Channel on August 1, 1902, once, after a tussle with a wave which pitched me about very considerably, my pilots lost sight of me completely for a time. Some minutes later they espied me about 200 yards astern, vigorously swimming back towards France. I was completely blind, and in considerable agony.

As most people know, in my later attempts I have used an air-tight mask, fitted with two watch-glass goggles, and this keeps the sea-water out of my eyes admirably. I would much rather, however, be without it, for after a few hours' wear it becomes terribly depressing.

I have been asked many times how I came to " turn up ' 24 hours' road cycling for swimming, and I think nearly every one will be sufficiently interested to learn the cause.

One day I met with a serious accident whilst cycling, and fractured my leg. When I recovered, my leg was very stiff. My doctor said to me : "Try swimming, old chap ; it may benefit the limb."

I took his advice, and to my great surprise became so fond of the water that the idea struck me to break records in it as well as on land. I have never gone in for quick swimming, staying being more to my liking.

Finally, I may say to aspirants for long-distance honours, never be afraid to " take it out " of yourselves whilst training. Hard work is good, and the more one gets of it prior to a colossal attempt the better.

Then when you feel " fit " slacken off and have a day or two " standing easy " before the big event. Then " Good Luck to You ! "

INDEX

Index

USEFUL INFORMATION ABOUT
HOBBIES and PASTIMES.

Carpentry and Cabinet-making

An Illustrated Handbook for the Amateur, with numerous Drawings and Designs.

By W. M. OAKWOOD.

Cloth, **Price 1s.**, *post free* **1s. 2d.**

This handbook contains a description of the tools most generally used, with instructions how to use them — The choice of woods for various purposes — Fretwork as applied to cabinet-making — A chapter on French polishing, staining, and varnishing.

Wood Carving
A Practical Guide for the Home Student.

By J. H. GARNETT.

With numerous Illustrations & Designs.

Cloth, **Price 1s.**, *post free* **1s. 2d.**

Contains—in addition to full instruction on the practice of the Art of Wood-Carving—Chapters on Choice of Woods, Tools, Designs, Appliances, etc., Chip or Notch Carving, Staining, Polishing, Gilding, Painting, etc.

Models, and How to Make Them

By CYRIL HALL.

With Illustrations and Working Designs.

Cloth, **Price 1s.**, *post free* **1s. 2d.**

The volume includes practical instruction for the making of a Steam Locomotive — Turbine Steam Boat — Electric Engine — Motors — Yachts — Printing Press — Steam Crane — Telephone — Electric Bell — Telegraph, etc., etc.

How to Take and Fake Photographs

By CLIVE HOLLAND.

Cloth, with 8 full-page Illustrations, **Price 1s.**, *post free* **1s. 2d.**

The Contents include :—

The Dark Room—Cameras, Plates, and Films — The Selection of Subjects — Exposure—Development and after Treatment of Negatives—Printing Processes—Mounting—Competition and Exhibition Work, etc., etc.

Metal Work

A Practical Handbook for the Amateur Worker in Iron, Brass, Zinc, Copper, etc.

By GEORGE DAY, F.R.M.S.

Author of " Handbook of Home Arts," etc.

With numerous Illustrations & Designs.

Cloth, **Price 1s.**, *post free* **1s. 2d.**

Some of the 16 Chapters are — Tools required for Metal-work — General Methods of Copying the pattern, drawing and transferring—General Methods of Working — To Etch on Metals —Fretworking in Metals — Useful Recipes for Metals and Metal Workers, etc., etc.

Half-Hours with the Microscope

A Popular Guide to the Use of the Microscope as a Means of Amusement and Instruction.

By EDWIN LANKESTER, M.D.

With Eight Plates.

Cloth, **Price 1s.**, *post free* **1s. 2d.**

CONTENTS.—A Half-hour on the Structure of the Microscope—A Half-hour with the Microscope in the Garden—A Half-hour with the Microscope in the Country—A Half-hour with the Microscope at the Pond Side—A Half-hour with the Microscope at the Sea Side—A Half-hour with the Microscope Indoors—A Half-hour with Polarised Light.

The above volumes may be had of all Booksellers, or post free from the Publishers,
C. Arthur Pearson, Ltd., 17–18 *Henrietta Street, London, W.C.*

Small Gardens

And How to make the Most of Them.

By VIOLET P. BIDDLE.
Cloth,
Price 1s.,
post free
1s. 2d.

A most useful Handbook for the Amateur. Full instructions are given for laying-out, bedding, arrangement of borders, vegetable culture, flowers and fruit, and trees, room plants, window boxes, etc.

Roses

And How to Grow Them.

By VIOLET P. BIDDLE.

Cloth, **Price 1s.,** *post free* **1s. 2d.**

The Contents include:—
Preparing Beds and Borders—Select Garden Roses—Planting Out—Climate and the Rose—Pruning—Budding—Climbing Roses—Pillar Roses—Rose Hedges—Roses for Shady Places—Roses for Towns—Rose Pergolas—Late Roses—Carpets for Roses—Rose Enemies—Roses as Cut Flowers—Roses by Post—Roses for Exhibition, etc., etc.

Greenhouses

How to Make and Manage Them.

By WILLIAM F. ROWLES.

With numerous Diagrams.

Cloth, **Price 1s.,** *post free* **1s. 2d.**

Some of the 22 Chapters deal with:—House Construction — The Heating Question—Working up Stock—Propagation—Pots and Potting—Soils and Manures—Watering—Shading—Tying and Staking—Syringing—Training—Pinching and Pruning—Arranging—Forcing—Critical Periods in Plant Life—Specialisation, etc., etc.

Rabbit Keeping

For Pleasure and Profit.

By GEORGE GARDNER,
With 12 Illustrations.
Cloth, **Price 1s.,** *post free* **1s. 2d.**

Poultry Keeping

And How to Make it Pay.

By F. E. WILSON.
Cloth, **Price 1s.,** *post free* **1s. 2d.**

The information given includes:—
Natural and Artificial Hatching—The Rearing and Management of Chickens—Housing, Feeding and Exhibiting Poultry—Breeding for Egg Production—Ducks for Profit, etc.

THE . . DOG

In Health and Disease
By F. M. ARCHER.
With 12 Illustrations

By S. T. DADD,
Cloth,
Price 1s.,
post free
1s. 2d.

Cage and Singing Birds

By GEORGE GARDNER.
With numerous Illustrations.
Cloth, **Price 1s.,** *post free* **1s. 2d.**

Some of the Contents are:—Birds for song, for exhibition, and for Breeding—care of young—Seeds, how and what to buy—Moulting for song and for exhibition—Colour-feeding; how it is done—Diseases of Cage Birds and how to treat them—Bird fever — Parasites and how to destroy them, etc., etc.

PRACTICAL HANDBOOKS ON
COOKERY.

Cold Meat
And How to Disguise It.
By M. G. RATTRAY.

Diplomé of the National Training School of Cookery.

Cloth,
Price 1s.,
post free
1s. 2d.

Contains a number of Useful Recipes for the Serving of Cold Meat in an Appetising Manner.

Little French Dinners

By EVELEEN DE RIVAZ.

("EVE.")

Cloth, **Price 1s.**, *post free* **1s. 2d.**

This excellent book contains Thirty Choice Menus, besides chapters on Savoury Toasts, the Use of Stale Bread, Seasonable Salads, Fancy Salads, Cooking Macaroni, etc., etc.

Breakfast and Supper Dishes
By C. H. SENN.

Cloth,
Price 1s.,
post free
1s. 2d.

The Recipes include Fish, Meat, etc., Vegetables, Salads, etc., Eggs, Omelettes, etc., Farinaceous and Cheese Dishes, etc., etc.

Dainty Dishes
for Slender Incomes
EDITED BY
"ISOBEL," of *Home Notes.*

Cloth, **Price 1s.**, *post free* **1s. 2d.**

The Contents include Soups, Garnishes, Fish, Sauces, Entrées, Removes, Vegetables, Sweets, Savouries, Artizan Cookery, Cakes, Food Calendar, etc.

Vegetarian Cookery

EDITED BY
"ISOBEL," of *Home Notes.*

Cloth, **Price 1s.**, *post free* **1s. 2d.**

Some of the Contents are:— General Remarks on Vegetarian Fare — General Remarks on Vegetables — Soups — Simple Vegetable Recipes — Entrées and Savouries— Farinaceous and Cheese — Eggs — Omelets — Curries — Macaroni — Liaisons and Sauces — Salads, etc.

Little Economies
And How to Practise Them.
By EDITH WALDEMAR LEVERTON.

Cloth, **Price 1s.**, *post free* **1s. 2d.**

Contents:—

General Management — The Financial Question — Kitchen Economies — Cooking Economies — Fuel, Firing and Lights — Catering — Home-made Jams, Pickles, etc. — The Kitchen Garden — Poultry Keeping — Laundry Work — Carving — Entertaining — The Servant Question — Spring Cleaning — Floral Decoration — Home Carpentering — The Sick Room — The Care of Clothes — Home Dressing, etc., etc.

The above volumes may be had of all Booksellers, or post free from the Publishers,
C. Arthur Pearson, Ltd., 17–18 Henrietta Street, London, W.C.

Amusement for the Home.

Tricks for Everyone

Clever Conjuring with Common Objects.

By DAVID DEVANT.

(Of Maskelyne & Devant, St. George's Hall, London)

THIRD EDITION.

Illustrated with 134 Photographs, showing the complete working of the experiments.

The Contents include :—Tricks at the Writing Table—Tricks in the Smoking Room —Tricks at the Work Table—Tricks at the Dinner Table—Tricks in the Garden—Card Tricks—Thought Reading Tricks, etc.

Fun on the Billiard Table

A Collection of 75 Amusing Tricks and Games, with Photographs and Diagrams.

By "STANCLIFFE"

2nd Edition.   Stiff Pictorial Wrapper.

"To say that no billiard-room should be without this joyous and ingenious little volume is nothing ; there is no player, amateur or professional, who would not get his money's worth out of it."—*Sportsman.*

The New Book of Puzzles

Up-to-date and Original.

By A. CYRIL PEARSON.

Author of "The Twentieth Century Standard Puzzle Book," etc.

Puzzle Editor " Evening Standard," " The Throne and Country," etc.

Fully Illustrated by Diagrams.

Containing Picture Puzzles—Enigmas— Diagram and Word Puzzles—Old Saws Reset—Tangrams by Sam Loyd—A Medley of Curios—Solutions.

Recitations for Children

A Charming Collection of Poems (chiefly *Copyright*) specially selected as being suitable for Young People, with instructions for Reciting.

By JEAN BELFRAGE.

To which is added Three Original Plays for Children.

Indoor Games for Children and Young People

Edited by E. M. BAKER.

In Stiff Pictorial Paper Boards.

The Contents include :—Indoor Games for a Wet Day—Games that can be played alone—Sunday Games—Games for Christmas and Birthday Parties — Home Stage Entertainments — Guessing Games—Table Games—Writing and Letter Games—Round or Parlour Games—Artistic Productions— Home Theatricals—Tableaux Vivants—The Art Exhibition—Forfeits, etc.

The Pearson Puzzle Book

A Collection of over 100 of the Best Puzzles.

Edited by J. K. BENSON.

The Contents include :—Simple Puzzles— Figure Puzzles—Trick or Secret Puzzles— Puzzles requiring Dexterity and Patience— Puzzles of a more Instructive Nature—Arithmetical Puzzles — Pictorial Puzzles — Wire Puzzles—Puzzles with Matches—Miscellaneous Puzzles—Riddles and Conundrums.

Plays for Amateur Actors

Containing Nine Original Plays.

Including Five Humorous Plays—A Suffragette Play—A Scout Play—Two Children's Plays.

With Hints for Amateur Theatricals.

PRACTICAL INFORMATION ON
THE CARE OF HEALTH.

Infectious Diseases
And How to Prevent Them

By Dr. ANDREW WILSON.

Price 1s., *post free* **1s. 2d.**

This little book is intended as a guide to the householder (and especially to mothers) in the all-important matter of the prevention of infectious diseases.

What to Do in Emergencies

By Dr. ANDREW WILSON, F.R.S.E.

Cloth, **Price 1s.**, *post free* **1s. 2d.**

The Contents include:—About Poisoning—Treatment of the Apparently Drowned—About Unconsciousness and Fits—Broken Bones and Dislocation—Things in the Eye, Ear, and Throat—Burns, Scalds, and Frostbite—About Wounds—Bleeding and How to Stop it, etc.

The Mother's Guide
To the Care of Children in Sickness and Health.

By LYDIA LENEY, M.D.

Cloth, **Price 1s.**, *post free* **1s. 2d.**

CONTENTS:—I. Pre-Natal. II. The Infant. III. Management of Children in Health. IV. Diseases of Children. V. Practical Advice.

"A book that every young mother should have in her possession."—*Health.*

Every Woman her Own Doctor

A Complete Book in plain English concerning the Ailments and Accidents to which Women and Children are liable, and their Cure.

By AN M.D.

Cloth, **Price 1s.**, *post free* **1s. 2d.**

The Author, a qualified physician of experience, has taken pains to distinguish between cases in which home treatment is safe and sufficient and those graver cases which call for medical advice.

For handy reference the whole book has been arranged alphabetically.

The Art of Beauty

By A TOILET SPECIALIST.

Cloth, **Price 1s.**, *post free* **1s. 2d.**

Some of the Seventeen Chapters are:—

The Cure of Stoutness—The Cure of Leanness — The Figure — Bad Complexions, How to Cure Them—The Hair in Ill-health — Moles, Warts, and Superfluous Hair.

Home Nursing

By SISTER GRACE.

EDITED BY

"ISOBEL," of *Home Notes.*

Cloth, **Price 1s.**, *post free* **1s. 2d.**

A practical handbook of useful instruction for the treatment of the sick and invalid at home, including Invalid Cookery, etc.

Indigestion
And How to Cure It.

By LYDIA LENEY, M.D.

Cloth, **Price 1s.**, *post free* **1s. 2d.**

Indigestion is such a common disorder that a book dealing very simply with its prevention, alleviation, and cure, should be very useful.

The above volumes may be had of all Booksellers, or post free from the Publishers, C. Arthur Pearson, Ltd., 17–18 Henrietta Street, London, W.C.

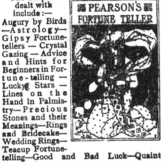